Short-Term Missions Success

Defining Moments Toward Long-Term Growth

MIKE LONG

Mike & Liz Long were appointed as UPCI AIMers in December 2013.
They went to France in January 2015 and were approved as
Associate Missionaries in August 2017.

ISBN: 9781521841150

DEDICATION

To Liz, Sophie, Dominic & Timo

…for the times I hid myself away in the upstairs office or wrote late into the night. Thank you for your love and your patience. You are part of this book and shining examples of what the Lord can do in lives dedicated to Him.

To Mom

The distance has not been easy on either (any) of us. You too have sacrificed time and proximity with family, realizing that the cause of Christ takes precedence and is worth the sacrifice. I honor you.

Aside from the Lord, you five are my greatest treasure.

CONTENTS

ACKNOWLEDGEMENTS

My earliest missions experience are thanks to Daryl Porter and Bret Robbe, youth pastors at Hillcrest United Baptist Church *(Saint John, NB)*. Their vision was picked up by an incredible church family that supported youth missions involvement without reserve.

For two years, in Belgium, I gleaned from Canadian Baptist Missionaries Dan Watt and Patrick Deneut and their wives. I was also very grateful for the support of Malcolm Card and Bob Berry and their wives, of CBM.

Since becoming involved in First United Pentecostal Church *(Saint John, NB, in 1995)* my involvement in ministry was encouraged by E.E. Goddard and Raymond Woodward, a strong team that set a fine example.

Working with Terry Kennedy and Brent Carter brought times of deep growth. I couldn't be more grateful for how God used them in different ways at different times.

I'm grateful for the John Nowacki and Paul Brochu families who invited us to join the work in France and for the personal support of Bruce Howell and James Poitras in UPCI Global Missions.

The love and support of Mission Point *(First UPC Saint John)*, the pastors and churches of the Atlantic District, our Partners in Missions, and pastors across the UPCI has been both humbling and a source of strength.

Finally to Darren Rowse, Chandler Bolt and Jeff Goins who inspired and informed both my blogging and eventually, my writing.

To God be the glory.

INTRODUCTION

I struggled with whether or not to include the term "Success" in the title of this book. How does one determine the success of Short-Term Missions (hereafter referred to simply as STM)? Are the results quantifiable? Some perhaps are but others are not.

One measure of STM success, in my opinion, is the long-term growth that can take place in the life of participants as a result of their STM involvement.

> "So then, let us [who minister] be regarded as servants of Christ and stewards (trustees, administrators) of the mysteries of God [that He chooses to reveal]. [2] In this case, moreover, it is required [as essential and demanded] of stewards that one be found **faithful** and **trustworthy**."
>
> *1 Corinthians 4:1-2, AMP*

Faithfulness and trustworthiness are measured in the long-haul. If who you are and what you do in ministry, partially as a result of your STM involvement, contributes to advancing the Kingdom of God in your own life and the lives of others, you're successful.

That being said, in order to experience long-term "success," your STM involvement itself needs to be as positive an experience as possible. That's what this book is about.

I believe there are steps that can be taken to ensure that your STM involvement represents extremely positive benchmark-moments in your life. If you've already taken part in STM endeavors you likely know what I'm talking about. It's definitely been my experience.

* * *

My first "Mission Tour" as we called them back then, took place in 1982 when our local church youth group spent roughly one week in Corner Brook, Newfoundland, in Canada's far northeast. We helped the local church by planning and staffing a Daily Vacation Bible School program, singing and testifying during regular and specially scheduled services and performing light maintenance work around the building. We became helping hands in a community that was not our own and worked alongside fellow Christians who, up until that time, we did not know. We were trained in service and grew in fellowship with the wider body of Christ. Some of those relationships carry on to this day thanks to social media.

Those STM experiences multiplied throughout my youth. Seven to twelve day trips took place annually, in Canada, the northeastern USA and eventually, in Monterrey, Mexico. At nineteen, I spent two months in Belgium and returned the following year for a two-year stay. Our family is currently serving in France and we have been here since January 2015.

It may be common to hear, but it's no exaggeration… STM has changed my life.

STM is … life changing ?

It's something that we hear all the time, whether in STM promotional materials of from participants themselves and as I've just said, in my case, it is true. Yet researchers in the wider Christian sphere, who focus largely on the study of STM say that significant, long-term life change is not the case for all STM participants. In fact, their research paints a dim picture of the long-term benefits.

In a nutshell, while promotional materials and participants repeatedly attest to significant long-term positive change, quantitative studies consistently tell a different story: Significant long-term positive change is the exception, not the rule. There are, however, key elements that can help encourage the chances that change, or growth, be both positive and long-term.

I'll spend the first several chapters speaking to you from my own 30 years of experience. The final chapters, in Section 2, is where I'll give you an overview of the material advanced by these researchers. I'll turn my attention to those key elements than can help ensure that your STM experience will buck what they see as the wider religious trend.

I did it. I bucked the trend. So I'm confident that the experience that the Lord has given me and my family over the past 30 years or so, will help you have an incredible STM experience and buck the trend as well.

Whether you are the pastor of a local church, a STM participant or a local church member, you have a role to play in ensuring that the impact of STM experiences are both positive and long-term: Truly life changing.

1

WHAT DOES STM MEAN TO YOU?

STM can mean different things to different people so let's begin by defining STM in the context of this book. Let's do that by answering W5 *(Who, What, When, Where, Why).*

WHO?

Briefly put, an STMer is someone who travels to a particular destination for the purpose of taking part in activities that flow out of Christ's great commission to make disciples.

STMers can be of any age.

More often than not we think of young people in their teens and twenties, but middle-aged people can take advantage of work vacations or a flexible work schedule to be involved in missions. Teachers often have 1-2 months off during the summer, time on their hands, and a wealth of experience to share. Retirees also have a role to play in STM. Finances may or may not be an issue for this last age group but if it *is* the issue, the strong backing of a local church can alleviate the concern.

STMers have varied skill sets.

Do you think that you have to be a preacher, a pastor or an evangelist to be involved in STM? Think again. STMers participate in a wide variety of projects. Some go with a set of specific skills (dental or medical missions, construction, etc.) but many go simply to be a set of willing hands, prepared to try new things and do "whatever their hand finds to do" or whatever is needed by the onsite missionaries or the receiving church. Typically the sending organization will work together with both full time missions staff and STM candidates to ensure the best match of opportunity and skill set.

WHAT?

My starting point considers STM endeavors to be an outflow of the Biblical imperative to make disciples; to build up and edify the worldwide body of believers, the church. My focus on church-centric STM involvement isn't meant to take away from the value of projects which are first and foremost humanitarian in nature *(eg. Teaching agricultural management, bringing potable drinking water to a village, working with inner-city youth, etc.)*. My focus is first and foremost an outflow of my own experience. Secondly there is only *eternal* value in those types of projects if they are connected to the gospel of Christ. Such projects then become examples of meeting physical needs so as to open the door to meet the spiritual needs.

STM job descriptions vary greatly. You could find yourself doing any of the following:

o Administrative Support
o Evangelism & Outreach
o Youth / Children's Ministry

- ○ Construction or Light Maintenance
- ○ Bible School Instruction
- ○ Helping Homeschool MKs *(missionary kids)*
- ○ Ministering in Special Services
- ○ Etc.

You could find yourself involved in any or none of these. Your job description will depend on what's needed on a given field, at a given time, by the sending organization and onsite missionaries. With this in mind, one of your biggest value-adds will be your flexibility. That being said, you can expect to have an idea of what's expected of you prior to leaving.

WHEN?

More often than not, summer is the busiest time for 1-2 week STM trips due to the overwhelming involvement of young people and their availability during school holidays. These are often gateway STM experiences.

As the duration of the STM project increases however – 1-2 months, 6-10 months, etc. – the "when" becomes more flexible and participants may find themselves leaving at any time.

A friendly WARNING: It is not uncommon that people "get bit" so to speak: They answer God's call to take part in a first short STM project (1-2 weeks) and they later want to repeat that experience and even go for longer timelines. More on that later.

WHERE?

When I think of STM involvement, I'm thinking of those activities that happen **away from** participants' home environment (this could be overseas OR in another area of your own country). The defining factor is that both the participant and the work in which they are involved is outside of their normal environment and comfort zone.

This is one of the values of STM – being outside of your regular environment, to experience and learn new things both about yourself and about the Lord; things that you can then bring back to your regular daily life.

Generally speaking, STMers are sent overseas or are working for a time in another part of North America. However, watch out for the perception that greater distance equals greater importance or a greater missions calling. There was perhaps a time when greater distance meant greater sacrifice but that time is largely past and all missions work involves sacrifice. The most important determining factor is not distance, or even the missionary that you might work with. The greatest factor is that you're in God's will for you.

God may be calling you to STM involvement overseas or he may be calling you to take your talents to a newly planted church in the state or province next door.

The question of "WHERE" also plays into the larger topic of God's progressive call. In my case, my teen years took me to Newfoundland (Canada), Ontario (Canada) and Rhode Island (USA) before God took me to cross-cultural opportunities in Monterrey Mexico and later in Belgium. The experience I gained on each of those trips built my confidence and my faith in God, which led to and enhanced my experience of subsequent trips.

God is in the business of building us progressively. Stay in His will and take things one step at a time.

WHY?

As I mentioned in WHAT?, I'm focused on those STM projects for which participants' main motivation is to express their faith through action. That action may be helping build up local churches, teaching and sharing their testimony or by "looking after orphans and widows" in practical ways.

Besides this most obvious WHY, another motivation bubbles beneath the surface for many participants. A motivation that you may not even be conscious of, yet it's there. Most participants are looking to change and grow, they're looking for deep purpose and they're looking for meaningful social connections. STM provides all of these and I'll discuss them in section 2.

WHAT ABOUT YOU?

This book is really geared toward three types of people:

1. Potential STM candidates
2. Pastors – who are a bridge between candidates and sending organizations
3. Members of the candidate's support network (church members, supporters & missions staff)

Let me briefly address each of you separately.

Are you a potential STM candidate?

If you are reading this book then there's something at work inside you. Call it a stirring if the word "calling" is a bit scary for the moment. Maybe you're wondering if God is inviting you to take part in a mission trip for the first time. Perhaps you've been on a trip or two already and you're wondering if God is inviting you to be part of

5

something longer term. Either way, keep reading. This book is for you.

Even a simple case of missions-curiosity on your part, should be explored and fed. While it may not always be the case, curiosity can be the start of a call. As you educate yourself on the various aspects of STM involvement, you will be better equipped to make informed decisions if and as the Lord clarifies a calling.

Are you a pastor?

You are the gatekeeper between STM candidates in your church and STM opportunities that may come their way. Someone who is serious about missions and wise in their approach will recognize the vital role you play. You can provide personal leadership and direction, out of concern for them, and you can facilitate the involvement of the local church both in terms of financial and moral support.

Beyond the time, cost and energy involved in sending STMers on mission trips, there are also benefits to reap in the local church upon their return. Your investment will help someone grow more skilled in Kingdom work – whether home or abroad.

Finally, positive, long-term change in the life and ministry of an STMer is not guaranteed after their return. In fact, some researchers are skeptical about the long-term value of STM. As a long-term voice of spiritual influence, however, you are in a unique position to increase the likelihood of lasting positive change taking place. If you maximize your position of influence in the 12 months following their return, you will go a long way in ensuring your church reaps benefit from the investment in that STMer (more on that in section 2).

Are you a church member?

Never underestimate your role in the STM process. Not only do you provide financial support to the pastor who has agreed to send an STMer, you also provide the moral support to that one who has agreed to go and a vital support to them upon their return.

While an STMer is on the field, you will frequently be the most substantial part of their support network. You've worked with them on a local church level, therefore you know them better than any other assembly. You know their strengths, but you also know their weaknesses, perhaps even their fears. God has been preparing you to uniquely undergird them while they're on the field.

You will also have an important role to play upon their return to the local church. You represent security and a safe place to exercise ministry, both of which they'll need as they come back with new skills, new vision and/or an invigorated faith in what God can do locally. You will help your pastor to ease their transition back to daily life. That transition is a vital part of ensuring positive, lasting change in the life of the STMer. You are vital to their long-term success.

8

2

MY STORY

In order to give you context for references I'll make throughout the book, let me begin by giving you the highlights of my own STM journey which began, in earnest, back in 1983.

1980s

My earliest church family was Hillcrest United Baptist Church (Saint John, NB, Canada). My mother had been involved in church from her youth. My dad, in those early years, attended more than he was really engaged (he developed a deeper walk later, while dealing with cancer).

Hillcrest was an incredible church with a very active youth group that was not content to simply receive. Youth were always encouraged to participate actively in the life of the church and place was made for them to do so.

Youth pastors, beginning with Daryl & Molly Porter, had the idea of involving the youth outside of the local church and in conjunction with other churches. Hence began a series of trips that would change my future.

The trips typically took a similar form. We spent several

months preparing a youth musical, consisting of 10-12 songs that would be interspersed with testimonies of how we'd been saved and/or how God was doing a new work in our life. This preparation involved meeting with the senior pastor to explain to him why we wanted to take part in the trip. Although approachable, this "interview" with the pastor was just unsettling enough to underscore the serious nature of what we were undertaking. It wasn't just about fun, games & travel (of which there was lots).

Preparation also involved writing out and learning our testimony. This may seem a benign element until one remembers that sharing your testimony doesn't simply roll off the tongue of your average 12-15 year-old.

In addition to the musical, we also came prepared to run a 5-day Vacation Bible School program, used by the receiving church as a summer outreach for children. Once that morning program was finished, we might sight-see or do light repair work around the building. Since "many hands make light work" we were sometimes able to help local churches with projects that they'd been putting off or simply didn't have the manpower to accomplish otherwise.

Slight variations aside, we took part in the following mission tours during my youth:

- Corner Brook, Newfoundland *(1983)*
- Burlington, Ontario *(1984)*
- Monterrey, Mexico *(1986)*
- Narragansett, Rhode Island *(1987)*

Do you see the progression? It speaks to what I say about the "WHERE?" of missions in chapter one. My first trip was in my own region of Canada, the Atlantic Provinces before going progressively further away, to Ontario and later Mexico.

Each trip allowed me to get out of my comfort zone, see God work both *in* and *through* me, and ultimately cause me to grow in Him. During our trip to Monterrey, Mexico, I distinctly remember the Lord telling me that missions – at least short-term missions – would be part of my future.

It's no coincidence that I had to get out of my comfort zone for the Lord to speak clearly to me. I'm not saying that God can't or won't talk to a person in the midst of everyday life, far from it. But I can say that there is value in getting away from the daily barrage of distraction, familiarity and the things upon which we normally lean for support. Without that familiarity we are more attuned to the still small voice of the One who is calling us.

On with the timeline.

In 1988 I graduated from high school and went off to Atlantic Baptist College (A.B.C., now Crandall University, Moncton, NB, Canada) a Christian liberal arts college where I did the first two years of a Bachelor of Arts. There, I was exposed to Canadian Baptist Volunteers (the Canadian United Baptist equivalent of the UPCI's AIM program). They were recruiting volunteers for two month STM projects in both Bolivia (South America) and Belgium (Europe). Since I didn't speak Spanish and was fluent in French, the choice was clear. I applied and eventually made my way to Liège, Belgium, in the summer of 1989 for a two month stay.

Never far from my mind was the word that the Lord spoke to me in Mexico, about STM being part of my future. While in Belgium that summer the Lord was tugging on my heart about coming back for a 2-year term.

I came home that summer (1989), returned for my second

year at A.B.C. and initiated the application process for a two year volunteer term. There were questions of fundraising, more interviews (ever as intimidating as that first pastoral interview in 1983) and other preparation to be done all while completing my second year of college.

1990s

In the summer of 1990, shortly before my planned departure for Belgium, my dad was diagnosed with colon cancer. For over a year he'd been undergoing treatment for something entirely different, meaning that the cancer had been growing unchecked. This threw the family into a tailspin, no one more so than my dad, and the question arose; "Are you still going to Belgium?"

I was.

I trusted that whatever would happen, God was in control and if I needed to return at some point, I could. There was no sense putting His will on hold for a question mark.

I lived and volunteered in Belgium from 1990-1992 and I loved those two years abroad. I made lasting friendships, saw God at work and watched him broaden my own experience of His presence and His Kingdom. In fact, it was during this time in Belgium that a friend of mine first made me hungry for the baptism of the Holy Ghost.

I was not unfamiliar with this experience as I'd had Pentecostal friends back home in Canada, but I always just sort of saw it as "the icing on the cake" or "the cherry on top of the ice cream sundae": The cake and the sundae were great by themselves, the icing and the cherry were really just "extras." My friend Freddy Decoster was someone who, at the time, would spend three to four hours each day reading his Bible and praying. I asked him how that was even possible, "I don't have enough vocabulary to pray that long" I said. To which he replied, "It's the Holy Ghost. When I pray, I go back and forth, praying in French and praying in tongues. That's how I can spend so much time in prayer."

He whet my whistle. For the first time I was hungry for that experience. I didn't see it as simply something extra, but something that I wanted for myself; something vital to developing a deeper walk, like that which my friend had. It wouldn't be until two years later (1994) that I would experience it for myself.

During my time in Belgium, we taught ESL and ran a weekly afternoon program for kids, both as a means of developing contacts in the neighborhood. We helped plan and staff youth and family camps, worked in weekly youth group meetings and helped facilitate national meetings. We were there both to support the national work and help grow a newly planted church.

I came home from Belgium in 1992 knowing that I needed to complete my bachelor's degree and start "adulting". I completed my B.A" in 1995.

The subsequent years brought much change.

I spent the summers of 1995, 1996 and 1998 touring French-speaking Europe with an inter-denominational Christian choir for two months each time. Again... STM was knocking at my door and I opened it willingly. It was during that first tour, in 1995, that I met Elisabetta Bennici. We married in 1997.

It was also during that period, in 1996, that I began attending the United Pentecostal Church in Saint John. Let me explain how that came about, not simply to digress or to tell a story. The process that brought me from the Baptist Church into Pentecost is a result of a poor transition from STM involvement back into regular life.

Re-Entry Gone Bad

I'd returned from the mission field in 1992 after being abroad for two years. During that time, a number of my friends had moved elsewhere for university while others had entered the full-time workforce or had married and begun having a family. Friendships that had constituted the core of my support network back home had changed. We had all experienced different things and the glue of common experience that held us together was a bit cracked and brittle. Genuine interest could carry conversations for a while, but we'd eventually hit a limit. What I'd experienced was beyond their grasp and similarly, their experience was beyond my reach as well. Since I'd returned and continued university I had a hard time relating to their changed schedules, their commitments and in some cases, their new circles of friends.

Additionally, the pastoral leadership of our church changed during my time away. The pastor who "sent me off" was not the same one that welcomed me back. We were completely unknown to each other.

When I was having a hard time dealing with the transition back to normal life (something I struggled with tremendously at times – there is a real grieving process) the familiar pastoral voice I needed was absent and while I could look up to a fine man who occupied the office of pastor, I didn't have the depth of relationship that inspired confidence enough to go to him for help.

I found myself roaming. Always in church and involved on Sunday mornings and mid-week, but roaming in terms of my activities, friendships, etc.; distance was increasing between me and my "first love." I was able to go through the motions while at the same time becoming lukewarm.

A friend invited me to the United Pentecostal Church for an Easter drama in 1996 and I felt something that I'd been missing; something that I recognized from my friend Freddy's walk. Over the following year I visited many times with increasing frequency, eventually making the church on Mark Drive my new home church.

A colleague from work, who also attended that church, became the anchor to a new social network and then assistant pastor Raymond Woodward invested time and attention into this young couple after we married in 1997. I found in him someone whose example I looked up to and with whom I had enough confidence to work through some of the things that had been taking me slowly off track since my return from the mission field, five years earlier.

2000s

After marrying in 1997, and starting our family in 2000, we continued to be very involved in our local church, First UPC, Saint John. We made regular trips back to Europe given that Liz's family was in Belgium and during one of those trips, we met missionary Paul Brochu who greeted me with; *"Well **that's** a New Brunswick face if I've ever seen one!"* I suppose being from Maine, he had experience dealing with New Brunswickers given the amount of cross-border shopping across our common border.

Missions remained close to our heart, so when missionaries came through on deputation, we were present. During missions conferences, we helped as much as we could and if pastor needed someone to host missionaries for a meal, our home was available.

In 2006 I joined the full-time staff of the church and in 2008, missionaries John & Anne Nowacki were through on deputation. They were not in Saint John on a service day but they were good friends of Ron and Joy Hanscom, our church's missions coordinator and former missionaries to Pakistan. The Hanscoms invited the Nowackis for supper and asked us to join them. During that dinner, on July 9th 2008, Pastor Nowacki invited me to come and teach for two weeks, the following year (2009), in the summer session of their Bible School. I went and eventually returned in 2010 and again in 2012.

Without knowing it, God was laying groundwork for an STM term in France that would not begin until 2015. Also unbeknownst to me, Liz trembled each time I went. She knew how much I loved French-speaking Europe and increasingly loved France. She had grown up in that part of the world and knew how hard people's hearts were toward the gospel. Her fears came true when, in 2012, during my two-week teaching trip to France, the Lord pulled unmistakably on my heart.

Bro. Brochu and I were preparing for a small Bible study with some university students. He was reviewing music, I was praying and the Lord was speaking. God's call was very clear: He was calling me to come back and be further involved in the work in France.

I largely kept it to myself for several months, with the exception of a small handful of people including the missionaries, my pastor and one or two mentors. I even withheld it from Liz for several months, not because I didn't want to include her or because I was uncertain of the call, but because I was asking the Lord to work on her heart separately from mine. In the end, I wanted her to have more than just a sense that she was following her husband to the mission field. He answered my prayer and gave me enough clues that after roughly three months, I spoke to her about what I felt the Lord was saying.

Every instance of God issuing a call is a bit different and the way it happened for us should by no means be "the bar" to which you compare your own experience of a call from God. If you are single, I daresay it can be a bit more straightforward in that you essentially just have yourself to worry about. At that point in my life, I had my wife, a 12 year old, 10 year old and a 7 year old to also think about.

I'll talk more about discerning God's call in the following chapter.

Liz and I let things simmer on the back burner for several months, not wanting to apply undue pressure. Then, in July 2013 we submitted our application for Associates in Missions (AIM) status.

We've been told that the application process took longer than normal for us, roughly six months. Having no prior frame of reference, we hadn't seen it that way and just assumed things were progressing normally. We found out in December 2013 that our application had been accepted and in January 2014 we announced our plans to the local church. We would spend the bulk of 2014 raising our support on alternative weekends, ministering at churches around New Brunswick, Prince Edward Island and occasionally in Quebec.

It's important to note that I worked extremely closely with my pastor, Brent Carter, from the time I expressed to him, (October 2012) the call I felt God had extended to us. He was aware of every step of the process from my side and was nothing short of 100% supportive the entire time.

17

This is all the more incredible given that he'd only assumed the pastorate of our church at the end of September 2012.

You will never go wrong working closely with, and under the authority of, your pastor when it comes to preparing your STM involvement.

Eleventh Hour Miracles

Our anticipated departure date, January 25th 2015, was fast approaching and it seemed as though on one hand, time was dragging on. On the other hand, it was flying by and a sense of panic set in.

- Our budget wasn't fully raised.
- Do we sell the house or rent it during absence? (we spent months going back and forth before eventually deciding to sell)
- We had to purge "stuff", sell or store furniture and decide what we would take to Europe.
- We were still ministering out on weekends.
- I worked full-time at the church through the end of December and trained my replacement.

Times of stress and panic are to be expected. If you wanted a low-resistance life, you wouldn't be contemplating STM! That being said, it's when our limits are tested that we find God to be limitless. Let me recount two miracles that took place at the eleventh hour.

Miracle #1: Timo

We were concerned by the fact that, though our two oldest children had experienced the baptism of the Holy Ghost already, our youngest, Timo, had not. We knew that time in Europe would mean far fewer children in church, far fewer Christian friends and far fewer children's ministry opportunities. It was by no means a paralyzing fear, but it was in the back of our minds.

We attended the UPCI's General Conference in Saint Louis, MO, in October 2014. During the global missions service, Anthony Mangun (Alexandria, LA) preached on how time and again throughout scripture, the supernatural followed the sacrificial. He invited attendees to make a sacrificial missions offering ($4.3 million dollars was raised in that service) and God was dealing with my heart.

For months we'd been undecided about our house. We were encouraged to *not* sell, so that we'd have something to come home to after our AIM term. On the other hand, we were being told that the house was uninsurable if the owner was out of the country (even though there would be full-time renters living in it). That all represented a great mental weight on us.

During that missions service, God put it on my heart that if we sold the house, not only would it lift that weight but it would also allow to make a sacrificial offering to Global Missions.

Pastor Mangun invited people to tell God what they needed in terms of the supernatural, whether healing, a miracle, whatever. I remember very clearly saying, "God I don't need a miracle and I don't need a healing, but Timo needs the baptism of the Holy Ghost."

Less than three weeks later, children's evangelist David Morehead came through for a regional kids' crusade and not only was Timo filled with the Holy Ghost on Saturday, but he expressed a desire to be baptized in Jesus' name and was baptized the following day. The most beautiful thing, no one had to tell Timo he'd received the Holy Ghost, not the evangelist and not us... he came and told us.

God had given us miracle number one.

Miracle #2: The House

As our departure approached, we grew increasingly dismayed about the sale of the house. Since we'd only decided to list it in October, it meant that we were trying to sell it in the weeks leading up to Christmas and on into winter – not the best time to sell a house.

Open houses were unfruitful and there were few offers. We finally did have one offer that was in our range so we accepted it only to find out shortly afterward that the buyer's financing did not come through.

Disappointment.

With no other immediate options at that point, we made arrangements with a property manager who would look after the house in our absence, working with our real estate agent until it sold. On the night before our departure from Saint John, however, we met briefly with our agent in the hotel lobby where we were staying. She brought a new offer letter from those same buyers who were able to get financing after all. The house was sold.

There's an old saying that puts it this way: "God is never late, he's always right on time." His timing is not always our timing, and for sure we'd have liked to have had that tied up earlier, but the main thing is... it was sold. God had given us our second eleventh hour miracle.

France

We arrived in France January 26, 2015 and have been here since, with the exception of one or two short trips back home (never all of us together). I'll end our STM story here for now although other bits and pieces concerning our time here may come out in subsequent chapters.

Summing Up

My STM journey, since 1983, has been nothing short of incredibly positive and truly life changing. Over the next several chapters I want to share with you some of the things I've learned through involvement in various types and lengths of STM experiences.

If God is extending an invitation to you to be involved in STM, I am thrilled right alongside you. If there's one thing I want for you, it's that your STM experience be as positive as mine, if not more so.

3

DISCERNING GOD'S CALL

There's a great tendency to idealize the call of God and to establish what it looks (or sounds) like. Is it the voice thundering to Job from the midst of the whirlwind (Job 38.1) or speaking to Moses from within the cloud (Num. 11.25)?

Of course the Lord speaks to different people in different ways. In my experience, Elijah running from Jezebel gives a good example of how the call of God came.

> "...the Lord passed by, and a great and strong wind rent the mountains, and brake in pieces the rocks before the Lord; but the Lord was not in the wind: and after the wind an earthquake; but the Lord was not in the earthquake: And after the earthquake a fire; but the Lord was not in the fire: and after the fire a still small voice."
> 1 Kings 19:11-12

God spoke to Elijah in the still small voice.

One of the things that I pray regularly, for my children and for others' children, is that from a young age, they grow to recognize the voice of the Lord. It doesn't come naturally, yet it's something that Jesus says will characterize his sheep: "My sheep hear my voice and I know them and they follow me." (Jn.10.27) We can't rightly follow him to that place where he wants to lead us if we don't recognize his voice.

Another example of the call of God that is meaningful to me is that of Saul and Barnabas in Acts 13.

> "As they ministered to the Lord, and fasted, the Holy Ghost said, Separate me Barnabas and Saul for the work whereunto I have called them." Acts 13.2

As they ministered.

A call to increased involvement in God's work has always come to me as I was already doing something for Him.

- I was involved in the local church as a teen and the opportunity arose to take part in mission tours outside of the local church.
- I was involved in 1-2 week mission tours in Canada, the USA and Mexico, when God told me that STM would be part of my future.
- I was studying at a Christian Liberal Arts college when what he told me in Mexico found an outlet in a two month STM opportunity in Belgium.
- While on that two-month assignment, God spoke to me about coming back for two years.
- During the late 1990's and early 2000's I was heavily involved in the local church and in French ministry and God opened a door to spend several weeks in France in 2009, 2010 and 2012.
- While there in 2012, God called us to be further involved with the work (without indicating a

specific timeline), where we serve today.

If you have a desire to serve God, it will not be limited to work on the mission field. Find a way to give your time, talent and ability to the Lord wherever you find yourself today. Work the task that the Lord is currently giving you (or the task your pastor has entrusted to your care), do it to the best of your ability (Col. 3.23), and do it in full agreement with your pastoral leadership.

A Call to Total Sacrifice?

Another idea we have about the call of God is that it involves total and complete sacrifice. This is true, but perhaps not always in the way we imagine it.

Do you think that it's not truly a call of God unless it involves snakes, jungles, and third-world or developing countries? If so, you may be incorrect. Not all calls of God are akin to that of Jonah, whom God sent to Nineveh; a place to which he did not want to go.

One of my wife's fears, each time I came to France, was that God would call us there, knowing how much I liked the country. Would God call us to a place we like?

Why not?

Trust me, you don't just wake up one day and, because you like a country, decide to uproot your family and move there. Yet for a call of God, we will undertake things that we wouldn't otherwise consider. Sure I liked France, but it would never have occurred to me to move there, outside of God's call.

I remember James Poitras saying one time, in a missions-themed forum, that if God is going to call you somewhere, he's also going to accompany that with a love for and a connection to the people of that place. Would God call you to a place where you would perpetually hate to find yourself? That wouldn't be very conducive to effective ministry, would it?

Has God given you a particular love for or affinity to a particular country, people group or linguistic community? It could be a clue.

Does that mean that God won't *ever* call you to a place where you *couldn't* see yourself living? I don't think so. Either way, let's not box God in to how he can or cannot call a person. My experience is an example of what Rev. Poitras expressed. In our case God created a "heart link" between us and France long before he ever called us to serve there.

Where to Go?

There may come a time in your missions involvement where God gives you very clear instruction about a particular place and a particular timeline. Until that time though, the choice of where to go may feel a bit more like guesswork and could be determined by practical means. Let me explain.

When it came to my first STM experiences, in the early 1980's there weren't ten different options available. There was one opportunity and my only decision was "Do I want to take part or not?".

When it came to my first extended STM trip (2 months), remember that it was purely a pragmatic decision. My options were between Bolivia (Spanish-speaking) and Belgium (French-speaking) but because I spoke French and not Spanish, my language ability sealed the deal.

My first 2-year STM term was to some extent simply a logical next step. Like Paul and Barnabas, God called me in the midst of my service. I knew the context, the language and I saw the need. In this sense, exposure bred an even deeper burden.

The "Exposure breeds a burden" concept also held true for France. I was initially invited for a 3-week ministry opportunity which was then repeated two more times. That exposure, over a number of years, was the growing medium in which the seed of burden began to sprout.

What About You?

Has God clearly called you to a particular place or a particular opportunity? If so, you are a bit ahead of the game. This usually is the case for those who have done multiple trips already or who have been entertaining missions for a longer period of time.

If God has not specifically spoken to you about a particular destination or if you're getting your feet wet for the first or second time, the question of "Where?" can be less straight forward. It need not be overly difficult however, if you keep a few things in mind. (Note: You'll find a short worksheet in the Appendix section to help you)

What are Your Options?

If you've not done an STM trip before, you should probably consider a very structured trip. In the UPCI context, Youth on Mission (YOM) and Apostolic Youth Corps (AYC) represent your best choices. YOM is organized on a district level and not all districts have YOM initiatives. AYC is organized by the General Youth

Division (GYD) and often brings together youth from across North America.

In these cases, your "Where to go?" options will be limited to the trips being organized for the current or upcoming year. Since there could be numerous options you need to consider a few other variables in order to narrow down your choice:

- o Do you have language skills that would be useful in one country more than another?

- o Do you have an affinity to a particular culture or language group (even if you don't speak that group's language)?

- o Do you know someone going on one of the trips? (knowing someone on the trip may not always determine your involvement, but if it's your first or second time, then having someone else you know can help you get your otherwise shy feet wet).

- o Has God spoken to you about one trip in particular?

If you've previously done an STM trip and are looking to go again, you probably already have a couple things going for you. First, you already have some experience in discerning God's will on the question of "Where?". Secondly, your experience likely also equipped you to consider longer, and less structured, options than what you have encountered to date (I'll touch on various options later in this chapter).

Unlike those planning for their first STM experience, your choice may be different. Having "tried your wings out" so-to-speak you may be ready to consider something different. You may be ready to "stretch" your wings, and your faith. The things you may need to consider include:

- o Do I feel God calling me to something similar to what I've done before or totally different?

- o Would I be willing to go to "country-X" even if no one else I knew were to be part of the trip?

- o Would I be willing to stay away for a longer time?

- o Am I willing to be part of a smaller team (eg. even if it was just yourself and a missionary family)?

- o Am I willing (or able) to get a two-month leave of absence from work?

- o Do I know enough about culture "XYZ" to be immersed in it for a prolonged period?

You may never have all the answers to your potential questions (if you did, it wouldn't require faith), but suffice it to say that there are more considerations for a longer, less structured trip.

Having Help to Discern the Call

If you're like me, you may analyze and reanalyze things "six ways to Sunday." Sometimes we're not the best discerners of the desires of our heart or matters of the mind. Sometimes we need help. Consider these two verses from Proverbs in the context of discerning a call of God to being involved in STM.

> *"Where there is no counsel, plans fail; but in a multitude of counselors they are established."*
> Prov. 15.22

> *Where no counsel is, the people fail: but in the multitude of counselors there is safety."*
> Prov. 11:14

Practically speaking, I've seen a call of God handled in two ways: very publically and impulsively or else very privately and with great pause for thought.

I happened to be in a service once (somewhere between the north pole and the south pole) where someone who had recently returned from STM involvement was presenting their time away, to the local church. During their presentation they boldly made the statement that they were going to go back within the year. That was several years ago and they've not yet left.

I tend to be of the latter persuasion. I clearly felt God's call in August 2012 but had only spoken of it to a total of six people in the three months following that call. For the following year or so, the only other people aware of it were those involved in the application process. Beyond that, our parents only found out in January 2014 (once we knew our application had been accepted) and then our home church later that same month.

We held our cards very closely to our chest, continuing to serve the local church while this new call quietly worked its way out in the background. I've always been a fan of discretion. It can save from embarrassment in the long run if things don't work out for any reason.

Who did I involve?

When I felt that God was speaking to me, in August 2012, I gave it a few days to work through it just myself and the Lord before speaking to anyone else.

Before leaving France, I had separate conversations with **Paul Brochu** and **John Nowacki**, the two missionaries in France under whose direct supervision I knew I would find myself. I thought it important to have a discussion with them, albeit a very preliminary discussion, prior to leaving France and returning home.

Once home and within a couple of weeks, I spoke with **Terry Kennedy**, the pastor I'd assisted between 2006 and 2012. It was he that had encouraged me, during that time, to pursuing ministerial licensing; formalizing the service that I was already giving to the United Pentecostal Church. He was an important voice in my life.

Towards the end of September 2012, a new pastor took the helm of our local church, **Brent Carter**. I had known him already and committed myself to work alongside him, for as long as the Lord allowed, with the same loyalty I had shown Pastor Kennedy. Within only a few weeks of that promise I let him know how God had been dealing with my heart.

In October 2012, I involved one final former pastor in the process of discerning God's will, **Raymond Woodward**. From the time I began attending First UPC, in the mid 1990's, Pastor Woodward had been a major voice in my life and knew me well. His was another voice I trusted.

Until I spoke to my wife in November of 2012, these were the only people that knew.

What did I ask them?

With a few exceptions, I don't recall which questions I asked of whom but here's what I was looking for:

1. **Their experience of God's call:**
    I knew that each of those men had felt the call of God for various tasks at different points of their life. I wanted to hear their accounts of

experiencing the call of God so as to help me ensure that I was accurately discerning his will.

2. **Objective 3rd party assessment:**
   In the case of former pastors Kennedy and Woodward, they had watched me grow as a Christian and as someone involved in the work of God in a leadership role. They knew my strengths and my weaknesses. I wanted their input as to how those strengths and weaknesses might encourage or hinder our implication in work on the field. Where my judgment might be skewed by either my love for the place or an overanalyzed and perhaps overemphasized awareness of my weaknesses, they could be an objective third party to help me get outside of myself so to speak.

3. **Their Blessing:**
   Although I don't think I phrased it that way at the time, I think what I was ultimately looking for was their blessing. I believe that blessing flows through authority and our willingness to work in submission to those authorities. If three of the most important voices in my life had any hesitation as to whether or not I might be suited to working in the context of global missions, it might have caused me to rethink things.

There's one question in particular that I do remember asking one of those three men. Let me give you a bit of context.

Fear #1: My (insufficient) Giftings

You know that there are different ministry types and skill sets within the body of Christ. Some people are good at teaching, others at preaching and still others at evangelizing or bringing new people to a saving knowledge of Christ. Soul-impacting ministry takes place when the five-fold ministry is at work and when spiritual gifts are present.

That being said, one fear I had was this. There are people who, when you think of them, you think of someone who "eats, drinks, sleeps and breathes souls." We refer to them as "soul-winners." It goes without question that all Christians are to be in the business of winning souls (because "He who winneth souls is wise." Prov. 11.30), but not all are involved in the same way.

When I thought of myself, I did not think of that person who eats, drinks, sleeps and breathes souls. Does that mean that I'm disinterested? Of course not. But I didn't see my primary strength as that of a soul-winner. To be honest, my predominant area of involvement in the local church up to that point involved more administrative and teaching abilities: the gifts of administration or helps (1 Cor. 12).

The question I asked myself: "Could someone whose primary gifting was not that of an evangelist truly be used on the mission field?"

I was afraid that my spiritual giftings, as I understood them, would be a hindrance, not a help, to work on the mission field. I somehow incorrectly understood that only those of a certain "gifting" were able to properly contribute to the work of missions.

The voice of my elder was soothing: "Mike, you are going there to help a missionary, to take work off of his hands so that he is freed up to do more of the work that God sent him there to do."

There was room for my giftings on the field.

Fear #2: The Context

The second fear that that same voice of wisdom helped clear up for me was one linked to the context within which I would go to the mission field.

The UPCI offers several STM vehicles:

- **AYC** (Apostolic Youth Corps): is a ministry of the General Youth Division whereby GYD staff plans seven to ten-day trips in North America and abroad. Young people travel to areas where UPCI pastors or missionaries are currently working. They may be involved in outreach services, evangelism and encouraging established believers. Without question, receiving pastors and church members look at them through eyes of respect as models of service to the Kingdom of God.

- **YOM** (Youth on Mission): These trips are similar to AYC trips but rather than being organized on an organizational level, they are organized at the District (or regional) level.

- **Next Steps:** This program is somewhat of a half-step between the 1-2 week trips and something longer. Combining three weeks of training and 5 weeks of apprenticeship, participants work with existing missionaries and mission teams to further the work in the host nation.

- **AIM** (Associates in Mission): This program is less tied to a specific duration. Some AIMers go to the mission field for 2-6 months while others spend much longer under AIM appointment. In our case, we will have been AIMers, on the field, for

2½ years by the time this book publishes. It is possible to stay at this level of appointment for even longer but questions of support and long-term financial planning come into play.

- **AM** (Associate Missionary): In the United Pentecostal context, this is the last level of missionary appointment that I would really consider to fall under the category of STM. Beyond this, anyone looking at Intermediate Missionary or Appointed Missionary statuses, are looking at missions less as an STM endeavor and more as a long-term project or even a career.

In considering these STM options, the most logical one for us was AIM. One thing I wasn't clear on, however, was this: I assumed that AIM was really only for people who weren't sure whether they have a call to missions or not and they merely wanted to "try it out" before committing. In our case, we had spent enough time in French-speaking Europe to know the context and I was sure of the call that God had extended.

"Was AIM right for my family?"

The elder answered the question for me: AIM appointment was not a question of confirming or validating God's call. Rather, it was simply an administrative framework which allowed the individual to serve God, for a prolonged period, in a foreign setting under the umbrella of the UPCI as a first time applicant.

If it helps to think of it in terms of a secular job, AIM was like the entry level position. There are certain responsibilities and benefits associated with it but there are limits as well. Think of successive levels of appointment as moving up within the company. You gain experience and skill, you get to know the company better and company leadership, in turn, gets to know you better as well. With greater experience comes greater knowledge, greater trust, greater responsibilities and greater benefits.

The example is perhaps a bit crude but you get the idea. By applying for AIM appointment I was in no way invalidating the call of God that I was confident in. I was simply going through the main door and beginning down the path of missions involvement. There was no guarantee on anyone's part as to how far we'd move down the path – maybe we'd get a year, two years in and discern that God's call was for that limited time, nothing more. We were simply now engaged down the path. We were able to get a feel for Global Missions and Global Missions staff were able to get to know us.

Speaking with a trusted voice helped to clear up two questions in particular, in addition to providing a good sounding board for more general questions as well.

Discerning God's Will When You're Married

Up until this point I've focused mostly on how I involved people *outside* my family, but if you're married, don't even think about engaging the STM process without involving your spouse as well.

With any ministry involvement, be it in the local church or otherwise, it's important that your spouse be supportive. Ministry often requires long days and numerous expectations. If your spouse has not totally bought in to that role, you can begin to feel a tug-of-war; if not in real life, at least in your own spirit; always feeling like you're trying to "rob Peter to pay Paul." In STM, like in any other ministry, balance is key.

If your home and ministry are in balance you will experience a greater sense of joy and contentment, and the effects are circular in nature. Contentment at home allows you to approach the work of the Lord in a better frame of mind. Overall joy in ministry allows you to reflect the joy of working for the Lord within your family. Without question, some days will ruffle your feathers, but with home-balance, they are the exception, not the rule.

As STMers, people will look to your family as an example. Like it or not, that comes with certain expectations. No one expects you to be perfect, but balance allows you to put forward a positive example of what it's like to serve God as a family.

You need your spouse to be on board. I'd seriously question the call of God if, after time and prayer, your spouse continues to experience serious reservations about STM involvement. If it truly is his will and you and your spouse are both spiritually in tune, then your spouse will either feel God's call as well or be genuinely at peace with what you've discerned God's will to be for your family.

What About Kids?

If you are STMing with a spouse, I've already given you two good reasons why that person needs to be on-board with your call and your plan. If, however, you also have children, the role of your spouse is even further amplified. If you needed them on board before, with children, you need them *fully* on-board.

Your spouse will be key in helping your kids adjust to a new culture and a new life. Change that might be manageable for adults can be incomprehensible for children. Depending on the length of your intended STM term, the departure can be explained simply as "a new

37

adventure" and embraced wholeheartedly by your kids. If you're leaving for a longer STM period though, that departure can represent a real sense of loss for your young ones and they'll need to grieve that loss. If your spouse is not fully on board, you will both have a hard time convincing the kids that the sacrifice is worth the "adventure".

Your spouse may also, at times, be key in getting you to slow down and remember to take time with your kids. It would be unrealistic to expect that one half of your couple can go full guns in ministry, leaving the other to totally manage the home front and have well adjusted kids. There will be times where your family will need you to take a break from ministry and just be "dad" or "mom" or "husband" or "wife." Your spouse will be key in helping you realize when those times have come and when other things need to be dropped.

If you are balanced, both as a leader in ministry and a leader in your home, then you minimize the risk of a STM experience being a negative experience for your kids. Who knows, it might be possible that one of your most important accomplishments, while on the field, is to plant a seed in the life of one of your kids for future missions involvement.

We have seen our kids[1] grow and flourish in many ways on the field, despite the absence of a traditional youth group support network. Without question, there are moments of loneliness, but in general they are doing exceptionally well, by the grace of God. I attribute that largely to the way that Liz has been totally on board with walking in the will of God and our having taken the time for that call to be cultivated... not rushed. There isn't a day go by that I'm

---

[1] At the time of publication, our kids are aged 17, 15 and 11 years.

not indebted to and amazed by her.

The Long and Short of it

The main thing that you need to take from this chapter is the following. The Lord doesn't always express his call in a thunderous voice from heaven, sometimes it's rather in a still small voice, heard in prayer, at an altar or perhaps even out on your morning walk. If you want to increase your chances of properly discerning the voice of the Lord, involve a handful of trusted voices in your decision-making process. They will help you answer some questions that you knew you had and may even help you answer questions you didn't know you had. Don't be afraid to address your fears during these discussions, the reassurance that you get in these conversations may help you balance yourself during times of doubt or frustration once on the field. There may be a desire or a temptation to try to know all the details of the big picture at once, but that's not usually how the Lord works. He gives us enough to take one or two steps, by faith. Once we've taken those, he will give us what we need to take the next step or two. We walk by faith.

Recommended Reading

If you are looking for further reading on the toping of discerning the call of God for missions, I highly recommend **"Sensing God's Direction"** by Bruce Howell and James Poitras, available at www.PentecostalPublishing.com.

In August 2012, on the day I felt God calling us to France, as soon as I got back to the hotel room, I went looking for reading on the topic of God's call and found this booklet. It is an easy read, filled with practical tips and will incite you to think beyond simply the emotion that can be associated with God's call.

"If you've got a call, Feed it!"
James Poitras

4

APPLICATION &
PREPARING TO GO

I've gone through a number of application processes in my time and it's logical to expect to feel butterflies in your stomach at different points in the process.

Think about the process for a moment:

1. You identify something that you want (eg. a car, a house loan, a scholarship) **or** want to be part of (eg. a university, a new job or an STM endeavor).

2. You fill out application paperwork.

3. Key players evaluate your application and discuss your strengths and weaknesses against selection criteria (what strengths or weaknesses will help or hinder the achievement of organizational goals).

4. Key players either end the process if they think you won't make a good match or they may invite you for a candidate interview.

5. You are either brought on board if the interview and subsequent deliberation go well, or the

process stops and you part ways if
incompatibilities become apparent.

I've been through such processes in both secular contexts
and in Christian ministry contexts, whether for ministerial
licensing or STM involvement. Following are a few things
I've learned along the way.

Apply Early

Note that, with AYC for example, even though trips take
place in the summer, application deadlines can be as early
as December of the preceding year. Don't leave things
until the last minute. I'd recommend beginning your own
personal selection process (where you might like to go) in
the October to November time frame since you'll also
need to speak with your pastor and get his input and
approval.

During our AIM application process, a number of
unexpected hiccups arose, that were outside of anyone's
control, resulting in a roughly six month process. Such a
delay (we are told) is unusual, but clearly not out of the
realm of possibility.

Involve your Pastor

This isn't the first time I've mentioned this (see chapter 3).
The fact that I'm repeating it should underscore its
importance. When you trust your pastor enough to involve
him from the very beginning, you loose his hands to be
involved in the long term project and believe me, there are
times when you will **need** him to be involved. Here are
several reasons why his involvement is not just
recommended, but vital:

1. **Responsibility:** Your pastor is responsible for
   you before God. You should make no major

ministry decisions without his input. He is also responsible for you to your sending organization. He puts his reputation on the line for you with STM organizers and you represent him while on the field.

2. **Objectivity:** Your pastor can help identify weak points, errors or omissions in your application. You want your application to be as accurate and as strong as possible. He is "outside of your head" enough to edit your application with objective eyes but still close enough to you to represent a "safe person" in terms of minor mistakes when completing the application documents.

3. **Experience:** Pastors often have insight into how departments, or individuals in a sending organization, tend to operate in terms of procedure, timeline, etc. He can allay fears and answer questions you have along the way. His experience may have given him opportunity to see applications that have done very well or which have been poorly received. You can benefit from tips he may have gleaned along the way.

4. **Networking:** If you have a good relationship with your pastor he may be willing to open up his network for you, in effect going to bat on your behalf. He could contact other churches or ministers himself or simply make an initial contact, allowing you to then contact other pastors directly, giving you a greater chance of being received. In some cases, due to ministerial ethics, pastors may be uneasy with you contacting them first, without going through your pastor.

5. **The Local Church:** If you are involved in your local church at a ministerial or a departmental level, your departure will leave a void in the

ministry of the local church. Your pastor will want time to plan staff changes or backfill positions so as to minimize the impact of your departure.

6. **No Mavericks:** Sometimes individuals wanting to get out of a negative situation find the idea of running to the mission field a viable alternative to facing and working through things. Avoiding negativity at home by "escaping" to the mission field benefits no one. The individual risks never really bringing closure and inadvertently takes negativity into their service abroad. Going through your pastor helps protect your long term interests as well as the interests of the sending organization.

7. **Membership has its Privileges:** In the end, you have no church connection stronger than the connection you have to your home church. The time may come that you will need that connection desperately. If you have faithfully served your local church then, more than anyone else, those people will be rooting for your success.

    -   If unforeseen expenses arise, you may need their **financial support**.

    -   Because they know you best, your strengths and weaknesses, they are best equipped to offer their **prayer support**.

    -   Because they know and love you, they will often be the first to go over and above with care packages and **moral support**.

If you've diligently worked with your pastor through the application and appointment processes, you greatly increase the chance that the logistical side of your STM experience will be successful.

Let me give you a personal example. As you already know,

I'd worked closely with my pastor from the moment he arrived at our local church, both in terms of day-to-day administration of the church as well as in terms of our STM calling. After roughly two years of working together behind the scenes, when the time came to make our plans known to the local church and beyond, my pastor wrote an open letter to all other pastors in our district (the Canadian provinces of New Brunswick and Prince Edward Island). He expressed both his personal support and the organizational approval for our involvement in France. He went on to invite pastors to either contact me directly or to go through him, as they desired, to schedule fundraising services or to make a donation.

This was a huge open door and a huge gesture of support. You increase your chances of encountering such a door of opportunity when you include your pastor from the very beginning of your STM process.

Finally, remember that once you are on the field, your pastor should be able to speak into your life at any stage. Your geography may change and the structure of your immediate team may change but your pastor is still your pastor. Leave him room to speak into your life.

Patience is Key

For my first honest-to-goodness adult job at Xerox Canada Ltd. I walked in with a resumé, filled out their application, did two hours of testing and had an initial interview all in my very first visit. Whether in the secular workplace or in ministry scenarios, that kind of timeline is not the norm.

My application for STM service in France was not nearly that quick. We submitted our application in July 2013 and got a definitive answer in December of that year.

Since we were applying to be furlough replacements for the Brochus' 2015 deputation, there was not a particular rush nor internal panic on our part. We were not phased by the delay in the least. In fact various players repeatedly offered apologies for this or that delay. I think that they were more concerned about the delay than we were. We were confident that we were in the will of God, confident that His timeline was working itself out and, in addition, we had no recent frame of reference to let us know how long it *should* take.

If there are delays along the way, remind yourself of this:

> If God has called you,
> God knows where you're at.
> God knows what He's called you to do.
> God knows when you'll get there.
>
> Then… just take a deep breath,
> rest in that knowledge,
> and do what he's called you to do in the meantime.

Tough Questions

Sometimes during the application and interview process, you may get asked some tough questions. Don't be thrown off by them. Two things on tough questions:

#1

Realize that a sending body engages its reputation every time they send someone out to the mission field under their umbrella. They have spent years building up a relationship with believers in various countries and establishing a work there. Similarly, those believers have put their trust in and have certain expectations of the organization. It's not unreasonable for them to expect that newcomers to the leadership structure fit in as seamlessly as possible. Local believers will see you as just that, a North American leader. You don't just represent yourself, nor do you even just represent the organization per sé, you represent the North American church.

During the interview process for my two-year work in Belgium in the early 1990's I remember a question, during the interview, that was doctrinal in nature. My initial response unnerved one of the ministers sitting around the table, leading to a series of questions where I was invited to clarify my answer. Afterward I was told that it had been one of the more grueling interviews and that they'd been tougher on me than they had been with others.

In the heat of the moment it was a bit unnerving because someone took my answer to mean something other than what I'd intended. If, however, you are able to coherently explain yourself, knowing that ultimately the people around the table want your best interests served, in addition to theirs, you'll be fine.

I don't mean to frighten you, but it's no small thing when a sending organization approves your application. It should therefore be of no surprise that they vet applicants thoroughly. Tough questions are in order.

#2

The second thing to realize is that "tough questions" aren't "trick questions." It is not in the interest of any sending organization to discourage those who have a heart for missions. Sometimes, in fact, tough questions can be an opportunity for ministry to take place. Let me give you a personal example.

I'd gone through two levels of ministerial accreditation (the UPCI's local license and general license) before being interviewed for ordination. I'd been working in full-time ministry for seven years by that point and was generally well respected. During the interview one of the district elders asked "How does your wife feel about you, as a couple, being in full time ministry?" (There had already been discussion, at that point, about our application for STM involvement in France, so the question also implied "full time ministry in France.")

At that point, I had a choice, give them what I perceived to be "the right answer" – "She's thrilled & couldn't ask for anything better!" – or be truthful – "She had some reservations." I chose "truthful" and proceeded to explain that my wife had always been faithfully involved in ministry in the local church and was an example in many ways. She never ever envisioned herself, however, as a pastor's wife, nor did she particularly envision herself living back in Europe after having grown up there. She knew how closed Europeans could be to the gospel and knew, therefore, what we were up against. "That being said," I continued "she did have a heart to be in the will of God and was confident that we were in His will."

Then I stopped talking and waited. Seconds passed (it seemed longer) and finally one elder minister, R.D. Foster expressed that what I was saying was not all that uncommon. "In fact," he said "God called Abraham, not Sarah, out of Ur of the Chaldees." If I recall correctly, he also went on to say that the wives of a number of other seasoned ministers (he didn't name them) would likely have expressed the same sentiment, yet they were doing a great work for God. In saying that, he calmed my fears and ministered to me.

If you are in the will of God, balanced in your faith and humble in your spirit, there's no reason to fear tough questions.

Administrative Preparations

There are many variables that would fall under the heading of Administrative Preparations so I can't possibly address them specifically. I can however, offer up a few things that I've gleaned from my experience.

Beyond the internal application process, there may be more or less complex immigration procedures that you'll need to engage.

Immigration

Depending on the country to which you're going and the length of your stay, it could be as simple as entering the country on a tourist visa and helping local missionaries while there. Never simply assume however that that will be the case. Some countries may require complex immigration formalities which take weeks or months to fulfill, whether you're going for a short or a prolonged visit. Between your sending organization and missionaries on site, they will be able to give you insight into the necessary paperwork. Depending on the organization, they may do some of that leg work for you or may expect you to do it from start to finish. Clear communication with all involved will ensure that you know the correct path to follow. Generally speaking, within the UPCI's STM program, AIM and Associate Missionaries, the expectation is that you are responsible to ensure that immigration formalities are completed. For specific information contact the AYC and AIM/Next Steps coordinators at General Youth Division and Global Missions respectively.

Housing

If your STM endeavor is only a few weeks in duration, or maybe up to a month or two, then the footwork for accommodations and other onsite considerations will generally be looked after – or at least begun – by the onsite missions personnel. The longer your stay, the more ongoing housing-related details you'll need to coordinate yourself.

Fundraising

Fundraising is without question one of the major parts of preparation for any missions undertaking, yet I won't treat it in this chapter. Rather, I'll dedicate the entire next chapter to getting people on board with your vision, for financial, prayer and moral support. On the topic of prayer, however, there is some personal preparation I'd recommend you do to increase your chance of having a positive STM experience.

Preparation in Prayer

In many ways we expect that prayer is a given. If you're sensitive enough to hear God's call to missions, it's generally because you've built up a relationship with Him and you regularly talk to one another. So it goes without question that you're likely praying in the lead-up to your STM departure, but let me suggest a few specific ways in which you can prepare yourself through this ongoing conversation with God that we call prayer.

1. Pray that God prepares you:

There are a number of ways in which you'll need God to prepare you for your time away.

Pray that God helps you learn lessons from Him.
- through time in His word
- through time in prayer
- through interaction with missions staff
- through national Christians
- through times of elation and even loneliness.
- through things expected and things that may catch you off guard.

2. Pray for the Nation he's called you to:

I once heard a minister say that what you see happening in the physical realm is a reflection of what is also happening in the spiritual realm. I'm not sure if that can be applied 100% of the time, but it makes sense to me.

In France, for example, there are almost daily reports of this group protesting or that group on strike. Rightly or wrongly, there is an attack on authority that goes back to the French Revolution where the people threw off the restraints of both church and monarchy... both of which claimed to be representatives of God to the people. Considering that unique history can inform how we pray for France.

The Lord has given you his Spirit to also discern things happening in the spiritual realm. Use what you see in the news, and what you know about the country of your calling, to pray. Realize, too, that since your are coming from outside of that spiritual climate, you may bring a fresh element of faith to the spiritual battle being fought there. If working in submission to local leadership, this can not only contribute to real change, but can also be of great encouragement to local believers and missions personnel.

3. Pray for the team you'll be working with

The more you are aware of their work, the more effectively and specifically you'll be able to pray for the missions staff and local leadership with whom you'll be working.

If they keep a regular blog, produce regular newsletters or are active on social media, subscribe to their updates and feeds so that you are regularly informed as to
- what they are doing currently
- what they've recently been involved with (noting any recent victories or disappointments)
- what their goals are for the work
- what new people are being discipled
- what new open doors are opening for them

Praying as specifically as possible for the leadership team with which you'll soon be working will allow you to slip into their groove as seamlessly as possible, making the team more effective, more quickly.

Pray, too, about clarity for all involved: Clarity as to your role and to the roles of other team members given your addition to the group.

4. Pray for the initiatives you'll be involved in

Prayers will be focused differently according to the type of STM endeavor that you'll be involved in.

Will you be involved in a **Christian based medical care ministry**? There will no doubt be a host group that has welcomed you and they will likely be involved in a local church or have services/devotional times among themselves. Take part in them and offer not only your professional skills, but your example of faith, worship and service. Pray, too, for people that walk through the door of the clinic. You may have an opportunity to share your faith with some of them, under the direction of your hosts.

Will you be ministering in **crusades or special services**? Pray for all aspects of those meetings, including;
- organization and preparations
- weather and attendees' travel
- support or altar workers
- worship leaders and musicians
- fellow ministers or speakers

Will you be teaching in a **Bible School or in ministry training seminars**? Pray that God gives you insight and revelation concerning His word and the ability to help you transmit it clearly to those in attendance.

What if you **don't know exactly what your role will be**? That's not all that uncommon believe it or not. When I accompanied a 2015 Apostolic Youth Corps (AYC) team in France several years ago there were days where they knew what to expect and other days where the plan was flexible enough to change rapidly and with little notice as a result of requirements on the ground. In those cases, go back to #1 and pray that God prepare you for the unexpected, so that you're always ready to give reason for the hope that is in you, regardless of the details.

I learned back in the late 1990s that one of the best words that can describe someone involved in missions is "flexible". If you can be flexible, and maintain a great attitude when faced with uncertain circumstances, changing roles and unforeseen situations, you will show yourself to be of great value to your fellow team members.

5. Pray for your Family

If you've done more than one STM trip or you find your trips getting progressively longer, your family may begin to feel anxious. Parents are thrilled to see their children following the will of God for their life, but it's often easier when the will of God has them staying relatively close to home. If God's will entails significant and long-distance separation, it can be tougher to swallow. Pray that they experience peace and have confidence in Him.

Cultural Preparation

It would be impossible to give you a list of how to prepare culturally for the various countries to which you might find yourself called. The list of countries is too great and the cultural nuances too many. What I would offer you instead is a few general recommendations.

I mentioned a few things when speaking of preparation through prayer, particularly praying for the nation to which He's called you. Familiarize yourself with what's going on in the country **through the news**, this will give you insight as to what nationals face daily.

Read about **the history of the country**. If there are significant events or trends in politics, education or religious beliefs, it would be helpful for you to at least have a basic knowledge of them. It can help you understand people's actions and reactions.

Ask your sending organization for a **Top 10 List** of cultural "must-knows" for that country to help you avoid misunderstanding or unintentional embarrassment. Your sending organization may refer you to onsite missionaries. To go one step further, take that Top 10 List and do further reading about individual items.

Use your network. If you know, or know of, other

STMers who have been to the country you're applying to, ask them what they learned or observed while there. Ask them what they wish they'd known before going. Similarly, if in your circle of friends there are people from the culture to which you're going to minister, ask them for cultural pointers to help you prepare. (Note: if they're not already Christians, it may open up a conversation about why you're going and be an opportunity to witness to them).

Be Flexible. This is perhaps one of the most important catch-all recommendations I can give you. If this is your first time in cross-cultural missions then you need to mentally prepare yourself for the fact that things **will be done differently** than in North America. It's neither good nor bad, it's simply different and it's how things predominantly function in that culture.

In North America, for example, our meetings (particularly special meetings or conferences) are often planned according to a schedule and, while still allowing God's Spirit to move, we try to stick as close to that schedule as possible. There are numerous cultures where time is viewed very differently. In some cultures for example, arriving 1-1.5hrs after the announced start-time is still considered being on time. If you go to cultures like these expecting things to work the same way as they do in North America, you will quickly become frustrated. Frustration will limit your ability to be used of the Lord to your full potential so learn to roll with it. Take your cues from the onsite missionary and by all means, don't consider it a lack of planning or poor communication on their part, it's cultural. Flexibility is your best defense.

Language and STM

Somewhere between discerning God's call, applying and preparing to go, the question of language always comes up.

If you are considering, or feel God is calling you toward a cross-cultural missions opportunity, you need to give consideration to the language question.

Let me start off with a personal example. In 2015 Liz and I accompanied the AYC France team (40+ young people and chaperones) during their 10-day trip. Their ministry involvement was primarily of three types:

- o Testifying, preaching and singing in services
- o Handing out church invitations in the street
- o Prayer Walks

It would make little sense for there to be a French language requirement for a trip of this length or type of involvement.

In service settings there was always someone available to translate testimonies and messages. They sang some in English and had learned a couple of French songs before coming.

When handing out invitations, one setting was in a city where use of English was common so they could easily accomplish the task in small groups, on their own. In another setting where English was not common, they were paired up with members of the local youth group ensuring a French speaker was part of every group.

Prayer walks, of course, provide no linguistic barriers.

Let's look at four factors that can drive language requirements in STM settings:

1. Missionary or Field Requirements

Ultimately, because any STMer works within a context and

an established authority structure, remember that the sending organization and/or local missionary sets the rules in terms of language requirements. What may work in one country may not work in another. In establishing a language requirement, the missionary or sending organization is keeping in mind two things:

o The best interests of the work to which they've made a long-term commitment. They know their constituents, the national culture and what works best for both.

o Your best interests as an STMer. Remember, they have likely seen other STMers come and go and have gleaned from each of those experiences (learning what they'd do differently next time, etc.). They want you to have a positive experience just as much as you do.

2. Type of Involvement

Obviously, the type of role that you will be playing when you arrive will be a key factor in whether or not you need to know the national language. Let me give you some scenarios according to various primary roles:

o **Evangelism & Outreach:** If one of your key tasks is expected to be daily contact with nationals… it's a no-brainer. You need to speak the language.

o **Administrative:** If your primary role will be administration work in the background (preparing course materials, accounting, cooking in a Bible School, etc.) then the missionary or organization may deem language skills to be of a lower priority.

o **Missionary Support:** I know one missionary who

began as an STMer appointed primarily to homeschool the missionary's children. In this case, not speaking the national language may not be a problem.

o **Building & Construction:** Teams often depart to assist in construction projects abroad. Language is likely not key here as long as someone onsite can liaison with locals (normally the missionary or a local pastor).

o **Mercy/Medical:** Here, participants are first and foremost bringing a skill to the mission field, medical or dental services for example. While they will have interaction with nationals, it will almost always be mediated by a receiving body; a local clinic, hospital, etc. meaning that the language can be mediated by your hosts.

3. Length of Service

I daresay that this will have some cross-over with #2 in that your role will often be impacted by the length of your intended stay. As a general rule, I'd say that the longer your intended stay, the greater the language requirement.

o **1-2 week trips** usually have little to no language requirement. Involvement includes conducting services, singing, preaching, testifying etc. and your contribution passes through a translator.

o **1-6 month trips** may have more of a language requirement but again, depending on your role, language skills may or may not be essential.

o **For 8 month trips or longer** you will come into increasing contact with nationals. The better able you are to communicate with them, the more enjoyable and personally satisfying your time will be… if not also more effective. If you're coming for a lengthy time like this and don't speak the language, you should at least consider enrolling in language classes on site or getting a personal tutor.

4. Your Age & Where you are in the Missions Process

Let's be honest, depending on #1, 2 & 3 above…

- o if you're 17 and are embarking on your first STM trip, you'll likely not be expected to speak another language fluently.

- o If you're 67 and going on your first missions trip; something you've wanted to do for years but are only able to do now that you're retired… you'll probably not be expected to have a new language down pat immediately.

- o If you're doing your 2nd or 3rd trip to a country and are considering a longer term commitment however, language should be one of your priorities.

Level of Fluency

Let me take a moment to address the question of fluency. There's a big difference between "I took courses in high school." and "I speak fluently." … one does not imply the other, however again, depending on the four factors above, fluency may be more or less important.

Regardless of how you perceive your level of fluency, once on the field, the key is to use whatever level you have to try to connect with nationals. They will be more impacted by your willingness to connect than by your linguistic ability. I'm often amazed at how some, with only minimal linguistic skills, are able to connect with and leave a huge impression on nationals. Why is that? Because their character and spirit communicates a desire to connect.

> *"Nationals are very forgiving of a lack of ability*
> *but they can glean very little from a lack of willingness."*

Whatever level of fluency you have... try your best.

To Sum Up

I've tried to show you what goes into determining the language requirement for various STM experiences but make no mistake, the more you're able to speak the language of the country to which God's opening a door, the more your experience will be rich and the more your time there will be effective.

In my case, back in the 1980s, language drove the choice of a STM experience. I had a choice between a two month term in Bolivia or Belgium, but because I spoke French and not Spanish, the choice was clear. I could be more effective in Belgium, so off I went... forever changing the course of my life.

Was I as fluent then as I am today? Obviously not, but God always takes what we offer him and multiplies it. My French ability grew and so did my ability to work in a French ministry context.

5

SHARING THE VISION

By now, you've felt God tugging at your heart about STM involvement, you know where you're going and your sending organization has expressed their trust in your ability to contribute to the work on the field. You're elated!

I say elated, but truth be told, you're both elated and a bit frightened at the same time for with one hand, they welcomed you to the team and with the other, they gave you a budget.

Ah yes, the budget.

As long as your plans remain in the "dream stage" things are relatively simple. You envision what you'll do and how things will go, your faith causes you to soar on eagles' wings. When the rubber meets the road however, you realize that you're not yet flying high but driving the long and winding road with the occasional pothole.

Your goal at this point is to get people on board with your vision. You need them to understand what the Lord has been talking to you about for some time in the hopes that they'll "catch the vision" and want to contribute financially to your mission.

This chapter is about how you'll communicate your vision.

My Experiences
with Missions Communication

Let me give you two reasons why I feel confident addressing the question of missions communication.

First of all, I spent six years as an Assistant to the Pastor in our local church which had an average Sunday attendance of between 275 and 325 people. Our people were particularly good about giving to missions and because of that, we often received requests for financial support. Both established and newly appointed missionaries and STMers regularly sent partner newsletters and/or requests to partner. Some were eye-catching pieces of literature that instantly spoke "quality" but not all were. When you put time, effort and thought into your communications materials, it shows instantly and your piece stands out in the pile. You want to be one of these.

Secondly, like you I have strengths and weaknesses. There are a good many things at which I'm only mediocre, the area of communications is not one of them. Time and again people have told me that my marketing materials and communication pieces are very good. In fact, there have been pastors who, without ever having met or followed up with me, began to support us simply as a result of our marketing materials. That is a blessing and I'm thankful for their confidence and trust.

I'm going to tell you how I communicated the vision, but let me start off by putting your mind at rest... you don't have to hire a marketing firm and invest tons of money to do it, that would be counterproductive. There are ways to produce quality materials fairly inexpensively and I'll share those with you.

Finally, if you intend to take part in a 2-week or a 2-month STM endeavor you may only want to incorporate elements of what I did, not all of it. Remember that we were planning to be away for at least two years. Later in the chapter I'll suggest communication strategy for shorter trips.

Let me break the following down into three types of communication: printed, electronic and personal or "in-person".

Printed Communication

This is perhaps the most familiar type of missions communication, particularly to those of my generation and older. Consequently it's one of the first go-tos when planning a communications strategy.

"Press Packet"

I designed what would typically be called a "press packet" in which I packed a number of communication tools, each with their own purpose:

- o **Intro letter** which
  - introduced us as appointed AIMers to France *(communicating organizational approval)*
  - gave an overview of our ministry involvement *(to inspire confidence in our commitment to service)*
  - introduced a desire to connect by phone *(to help move us beyond "just another letter in the pile")*
  - detailed the contents of the packet *(so they wouldn't miss anything)*

- was signed by myself and my pastor
(communicating pastoral awareness & approval)

o A **branded postcard** (more on branding below) with a personalized, handwritten note on the back. I wanted to make a personal connection with each pastor to which I was writing (over 200 – from our region, from personal connections or based on recommendations). That's a lot of handwritten notes, but never underestimate the power of personal in a world where electronic communication and form letters are the norm.

How did I personalize the notes?

With churches from the region, or with established personal connections, personalization was fairly simple. For churches and pastors that I didn't already have a personal connection with, I perused their website looking for something in common.

I designed the postcards and printed them at VistaPrint.com. Their downloadable templates facilitate the initial design parameters and they are not expensive.

o **Two printed bookmarks**, the front of which showed and named our family and indicated the general nature of our AIM appointment: furlough replacements for missionaries. The back of the bookmark gave the website address for our blog and invited them to partner with us.

Again, I designed the bookmarks but this time had them printed at PrintSafari.com (VistaPrint doesn't do bookmarks).

The **purpose** of the bookmark was an attempt to gain "mindshare" (an ongoing level of awareness about us as AIMers and the work that we're involved in). I encouraged them to place it in their Bible or in a place where they'd see it regularly to remember to pray for us. The more "mindshare" you have, the more prayer support and possibly financial support you stand to raise.

o Our **Partner in Mission** (PIM) **form**. For those pastors who were immediately prepared to support us financially, I didn't want to give them a reason to "put off" making the decision. If they wanted to support us but had to contact me for a PIM form there's a chance that they'd get distracted and forget about it for a time or forget about it all together. Remove barriers for making a decision.

o A printed "**France at a Glance: AIMKids Edition**" **Infographic** was included in a later mailing as well. It was intended to be directed to Sunday School & Youth Directors as it focused on our kids in particular. It included:

- Their photos, birth dates and interests
- Points on how to pray for and encourage them *(for example if a Sunday School class wanted to adopt them as an ongoing missions "project")*
- 7 fun facts about France and our life here *(again, an attempt to make it engaging for kids)*
- Our website address and Global Missions account number.
- An encouragement that when they prayed for missions, they were part of missions too!

Again, the goal with this piece was simply to get our names, locations and project out and into the hands and minds of as many people as possible, in a visually pleasing way.

This infographic was made using **Piktochart.com**. It is a paid membership site but they have special pricing for Not-for-Profit organizations. If it's something that your church could use on an ongoing basis, your pastor or office administrator may consider subscribing and allowing you access to develop similar tools.

o A link to an **introductory 10-min video** on our website: AIMLong.ca/video (it has since been replaced with a shorter video) There is only so much information that can be communicated by letter (avoid exceeding one page if possible), yet I wanted to put more information out there for those pastors who would desire more before making a decision. In that video I introduced the work in France, the missionary team and the work that we anticipated doing. I highlighted our prior involvement in the work there and had a short video endorsement from a previous pastor.

Another thing I'd consider printed communication, although it's not something I included in mail-outs, is articles in organizational or district publications. Editors are sometimes looking for content and if you can offer them something engaging and visually appealing, they may be open to publishing your article.

Once, we also paid for advertising in a district publication. Although providing an article incurred no expense, paying for content allowed us to have the back cover, printed in color – prime real-estate for readership.

Branding & Printed Communication

The word "marketing" can be met with skepticism when it refers to the work of God, but in essence, anytime you're promoting your vision, you're engaged in marketing.

A key idea in marketing is "branding" or making your

communication both instantly recognizable and engaging. To that end our communication pieces followed the same branding principles:

- o Always featuring **key graphic elements**: the same family photo, the same photo of Liz & I or the same map of France.

- o Consistently using the **same colors** and **fonts**.

- o Graphic elements were incorporated into a **letterhead**, for consistency of communication.

- o **Mailing labels** featured our website address and mailing address, using the main color scheme.

I've created a hidden page on my website to show you images of the various tools that I mention in this first section. Go to: AIMLong.ca/STMScommunication

Let's move from printed communication (typically more costly), to electronic communication which has the advantage of broad distribution for minimal cost.

Electronic Communication

Since coming to the field, our printed communication has diminished greatly in favor of online communication – primarily due to associated costs – though I still send out handwritten notes from time to time as a way to connect personally. Here's a look at what we've done online:

Website / Blog

By far our most regular form of communication is through our website: **AIMLong.ca**. built on the Wordpress.COM[2]

platform, which began strictly as a blogging platform but is now a great deal more. I HIGHLY recommend Wordpress.com!

I wanted the website to be a "one-stop shop" for anything relating to our STM term abroad. Information on AIMLong.ca can largely be grouped into two categories:

1. **Information Central:** Again, there's only so much information that can be sent via printed format. Some potential supporters will want a minimal amount, some will want more. Here's what I make available:

    a. Background on our calling and prior involvement with the work in France and French ministry in general.

    b. The type of work that we expected to be involved in (as we knew it at the time and updated as it evolved).

    c. The financial needs associated with our AIM appointment along with a downloadable copy of our PIM form and instructions on completion & submission for both Canadian and US donors. (Again, make it easy so that if they decide to support you, everything they need is

---

[2] **Note:** Wordpress.COM is the free, hosted version of Wordpress and in my opinion the easiest for what STMers will need it for. Don't confuse it with Wordpress.ORG for which you will have to purchase hosting separately and maintain multiple plugins. Basic Wordpress templates are free while premium templates, although they have an one-time associated cost, generally have more flexibility. If you choose a premium Wordpress account (minimal annual cost) it allows you to associate a dedicated domain name and eliminates the random placement of ads on your blog.

easily accessible).

d. Information on our kids, the goal being to not only encourage regular prayer for them but also to provide kid-themed 5-minute lessons for use in Sunday School settings (AIMLong.ca/Kids). Each one presents a French-themed object lesson that gets kids thinking about missionary kids in France and on how *they* can be missionaries in their own town or school.

2. **Regular Updates:** For established and potential partners (but also for friends and family) we also have a blog portion of the site (Wordpress' core competency): AIMLong.ca/Blog.

    We publish posts weekly, each one in the 500-1,000-word range. Enough to provide highlights in about the time required to drink a cup of coffee. The posts also publish automatically to our Facebook page (Facebook.com/AIMLongFrance) as well as my personal Twitter feed.

Facebook

Let me state from the outset that Facebook is not my preferred method of communication. I'm there because it *is* a regular communication platform for 79% of internet users, according to a 2016 Pew Research study. That number includes many of our supporting pastors and individual supporters. Some are more accessible on Facebook, for example, than they are via email.

I have a personal profile and a Facebook page for our AIM work (Facebook.com/AIMLongFrance) and while I generally try to keep the two separate, cross-over inevitably happens periodically.

In an attempt to balance the need to *be* on Facebook (for effective networking) while at the same time limiting my time *on* Facebook, I configured all new posts to automatically publish directly to the Facebook page. From time to time I interact directly (if and when comments are made or people are interacting with the page) but not overly frequently.

Over and above a publishing platform, Facebook is also convenient in terms of direct messaging, making for easy and rapid communication.

Email Updates

Despite publishing weekly on AIMLong.ca and relaying published posts to Facebook and Twitter, I'm sensitive to the fact that not everyone will be online at the right time to see my posts (particularly with Facebook's ever changing algorithms which wreak havoc on readership). For this reason, I also produce regular newsletters that go directly to supporter's inboxes via email.

Amid several possible email service providers we use MailChimp.com because it is free to use until you reach a certain volume of email traffic (STMers generally don't have to worry about hitting that ceiling).

The platform allows you to easily build and send customized emails (including colored text, various fonts, images, video links and Call-to-Action buttons) directly to subscribers. You can get a subscription link for use online which even provides reports on delivery, opens, clicks, etc.

It's a powerful tool that allows you to easily manage the various tasks required to successfully manage email communication to a subscriber base.

Twitter

Although I've mentioned Twitter a number of times, I don't use it extensively or exclusively for STM promotion. New blog posts publish automatically to my personal Twitter feed and that's about the extent of my use in terms of STM.

Though I don't push my Twitter use really hard, I regularly see traffic come to my blog from there, so remember, even if you don't use it extensively, many of the pastors that you'd like to connect with, do.

Other Social Media

There are of course other social media platforms that can be used to promote your STM involvement. To date I've mentioned the ones that I used most.

I don't use the following for STM promotion, but others do use them with varied levels of success:

- ○ **Pinterest:** Primarily image based, if you enjoy or are good at creating sharable images and are looking to communicate with a predominantly feminine base, Pinterest may be worth considering.

- ○ **Instagram:** More and more churches are using Instagram to connect with members and the general public. There's no reason why you couldn't also capitalize on this audience.

- ○ **Snapchat:** Know that the user base for this social media platform is primarily a younger crowd (teens and twenties). Like any social platform, if it has the potential to get your message out in front of an audience it's worthy of your consideration.

There are no doubt more social media platforms I could mention and surely some that other STMers are using but it can feel overwhelming to consider them all and I'd strongly advise against it.

My advice is to choose one or two to start with. If you're able to add others, do so, but don't feel obliged. If you get to the point where you spend more time managing social media than ministering, you're out of balance.

Online Video

The idea of putting together a short introductory video should not be an intimidating proposition. It's easy to film something of decent video quality with the smartphone you carry with you at all times. Given current video trends, gone is the expectation that videos be filmed in studio with steady footing; handheld and movement is increasingly acceptable (within reason of course). Here are my recommendations:

- o If possible have your smartphone on a small tripod or propped on a flat surface.
- o Dress in business casual attire.
- o Keep your video to 2-5 minutes in length (3 is ideal).
- o Purchase or borrow a lavalier mic for quality sound (if not possible, just stay close to the built-in mic).
- o A number of editing apps are available if needed.
- o Online tools such as Lumen5.com can help you put together imaged-based video in a matter of minutes with captions, royalty-free images and music.

Branding and Electronic Communication

I already discussed what branding looked like for printed communication, the basic principle remains the same for electronic communication: "consistency in look."

Ideally, the "look" will be consistent across all of your communication tools (printed and electronic), that can be accomplished by colors and key graphics. Fonts reproduction may be a bit more difficult depending on the electronic platform that you use, but it's rarely impossible.

Based on my Wordpress template for example, I am always consistent in heading styles, fonts and highlight colors. The way I use photos is also consistent (always with a drop shadow and usually tilted).

From there I take images that I develop for the website and adapt them for use on other online platforms like social media. In this way, my online presence is consistent.

Personal Communication

The final way that you communicate your vision is in person. This can happen when you are invited to share your vision at a neighboring church, sitting across the desk from a pastor or across the table from a friend, a family member or a business colleague.

When visiting another church, the pastor may ask if you have any kind of a missions display or materials to distribute. If that's the case, you can pull out some of the printed materials that I mention above. Note that it's always a good idea to ask the pastor how *he* would prefer that any distribution of print pieces take place. Some have definite preferences.

The only other thing I'd recommend having with you, if possible, is some kind of eye-catching display piece. In my case I used a vertical banner that measured roughly 6' x 2'.

It adhered to my branding (colors, fonts, key images and messaging) and made a positive impression. You can often have such banners printed at Staples or FedEX Office stores for less than $100.00.

I've listed a few extra resources below that are rich resources in the area of personal communication and people raising. Suffice it to say that if you are in God's will and confident in His vision, then simply communicate that and don't be afraid to ask for a financial commitment.

"The door is opened to him who knocks and he who asks shall receive."

Recommended Resources

On the subject of fundraising and communication I'd like to point you to the following resources:

On Fundraising:

- **The God Ask**, by author Steve Shadrach (2013), is an incredible resource. He starts from the premise that God has already prepared people who both believe in you and/or who will believe in the cause you are promoting, you just have to go find them. Nehemiah's relationship with King Artaxerxes allowed him to approach the King with regards to rebuilding Jerusalem. The King's response? "Here's a blank cheque."

- **www.JennFortner.com** is another resource with great material. Her blog, **Financial Partnership Development: Fundraising Made Relational**, features lots of Jenn's own posts as well as guest posts from other successful fundraisers. She works as a fundraising coach for Assembly of God Eurasia Missionaries.

- Two other websites/blogs worth mentioning here are **PeopleRaising.com/people-raising** and **SupportRaisingSolutions.org/blog**. While they have products available for purchase, there are ample amounts of free content available as well.

On Communication:

Two STMers who have come through the UPCI's AIM program, and are currently serving as Associate Missionaries, do an exemplary job with communication.

- **Baron & Jen Carson** are currently located in the Netherlands and excel at a combined use of their own blog (**www.HopeForHolland.com**) and social media for keeping their support network up to date. Baron makes very effective use of video content.

- **Daniel & Christine Patterson** are currently serving in Romania. Daniel blogs regularly at **NavigateMissions.wordpress.com** in addition to communicating monthly via email, with the dependability of a Swiss watch.

I'd recommend subscribing to the update feeds of both of these Associate Missionary couples to begin getting a sense of how they communicate. Let yourself be inspired and then incorporate what you are able to bring into your own communication efforts.

To help you get started, I've included a checklist in the appendix section at the back, of what I'd recommend you start with.

Final Tips on Communication

- One picture that tells a great story is better than posting the last 35 photos from your camera roll.

- Strike a careful balance between being "open and transparent" and being negative and critical. Words can be taken out of context so you don't want to publicly mention anything that could be twisted to reflect poorly on your sending organization, your missions colleagues or ultimately, the Lord. (Remember, depending on your social media privacy settings, that comment you just tweeted isn't only available to Christian friends, but may be visible to people you're trying to minister to as well.).

- People's reading attention span is constantly becoming shorter and there's more a tendency to "scan" than to "read" so limit reports in length and amount of detail. When in doubt, keep it short, sweet and to the point.

- If you share specific prayer requests, follow-up and tell supporters how the Lord answered prayer. Keep them feeling included.

- Writing 2-3 paragraphs every week/month is better than writing 3,000 words once every six months... it's the concept of "pinging" ... regular, short connect points, each of which reaffirm the relationship.

- Just because you have a blog, doesn't mean people will flock to it. Don't assume people will always come to you... rather, be sure that you're going to them with news (email, Facebook, Twitter, etc.)

- Proof read all communications. When you're finished… proof read again. If possible, get someone else to do it for you… they'll almost always catch something that would otherwise have gotten through.

How to Communicate for
Shorter STM trips?

At the outset I mentioned that the extensiveness with which we approached communication was in anticipation of a 2-year stay overseas. If you are only planning to be away for a couple of weeks or even a couple of months, an attempt to incorporate all the things I've mentioned here would be overkill. Let me give you my recommendation for what to include for shorter STM assignments (you can also reference the Communications Checklist at the back of the book):

2 Weeks

Your communication goal for a short time away is to raise awareness, raise support in the form of one-time donations and to enlist prayer partners during your time away. For this purpose I'd recommend at least the following.

- o Have an introduction letter for potential supporters *(including any social media channels you intend to use)* including pastoral endorsement.
- o Have a service where you can present your burden to the local church, with your pastor's approval.
- o Post daily updates via social media while away.
- o Have a dedicated hashtag for social media posts.

2 Months +

- o All of the above, *plus…*

o Update to a blog or a dedicated Facebook Page. In addition to your personal profile as well.
o Have a bookmark or prayer card to put in the hands of supporters as a daily reminder.
o Seek out opportunities to "cast a wider net" than simply your home church (with the accord of your pastor). For example,
   ▪ Post an online introductory video.
   ▪ Initiate discussions – via your pastor – about presenting your burden to other churches.
   ▪ Offer to submit an article to a district publication.

As a final word let me say this. Fundraising is an important goal of communication, but an even bigger goal is to make people feel that they are part of accomplishing the great commission. Communicating vision lifts their faith as well.

"Some give by going,
others go by giving."

Communicating is about taking others with you! If you can successfully do that, the finances will follow.

6

MISTAKES TO AVOID

Based on some of the research that I'll detail further starting in chapter ten, along with my own experience, let me offer up eight common mistakes that can ultimately make your STM experience less than the best experience possible.

1. Participant Clustering

More often than not, STM is about the coming together of two groups: North American participants and host country nationals. Depending on the type of work you'll be involved with, interaction between the two groups may be extensive or fairly limited. It's possible that you'll only attend services with them once or twice during your stay or you may find yourself working very closely to them on a project.

Regardless of the context, a separation often begins to take place. You interact with nationals, smile, exchange pleasantries, perhaps even share in a few more involved discussions. You lean in close and listen intently, trying to navigate their broken English or perhaps a thick accent.

Maybe you need to ask them once or twice to repeat their last statement. On the third time, though still didn't quite get it, you refrain from asking them to repeat once more, not wanting to offend them or make it clear that you still didn't quite understand.

Contrast that to the conversation that you have back in the bus, with a team member from a neighboring state or province. Sure you may tease them about their Maine, Texas, Alabama or Newfoundland accent, but you really have no trouble understanding them. You share the same cultural references and tend to assume a more relaxed posture when talking with them. Let's face it, communication within the team is often a whole lot easier and if your mind is tired from straining to understand nationals, there can be a sense of relaxed relief when you get to just be together as a team.

The longer you're on the field the greater the bonds that form between you and your teammates and the easier it becomes to slip into those North American conversations. An unintentional consequence of that intra-team ease is that unstructured yet focused time spent with nationals decreases. This is the point at which participant clustering begins to become evident.

The Plus: You're developing friendships with likeminded individuals that have a greater chance of carrying on with you, into the future, once back in North America.

The Minus: You limit opportunities to gain outside perspective and cross-cultural insight; things that you so looked forward to when planning the trip.

What's at stake? You have the opportunity to make a deposit into the life of a believer in another country. Who knows but that, like Esther, you were brought to the mission field for this very reason: to speak into the life of one of the nationals that God will put you in contact with. Regardless of how *you* see yourself, they see you as Kingdom of God royalty. They expect to learn from you and from your example. Similarly, who knows what you might gain by connecting with them or what you might miss out on by not doing so.

The Antidote: When you have opportunity, make a point to engage nationals in conversation. Opportunities like sitting together for a meal, a snack or a coffee break are great chances to connect. If you're shy, grab another team member to go with you. If you're not sure where to begin a conversation with nationals, ask them about:

- How long they've been in church.
- How they came to walk with the Lord.
- What they were most looking forward to during the time that they'd spend with the team.
- How they're involved in their local church.
- What they most enjoy about serving the Lord.

> *"An attitude of openness,*
> *not language,*
> *is the most important factor*
> *in communication."*

2. Shared Learning

This second "mistake" falls on the heels of the first and underscores the importance of interaction between STMers and receiving churches, pastors and individuals.

As you go to the field, you have something worth sharing with the people among whom you'll be working. If you didn't believe this, you likely wouldn't be going. Nationals anticipate your arrival and they fully expect to glean from your time with them; expecting to learn both from any formal teaching or sharing that you'll be involved in as well as informally, from your example.

Invariably, STMers return from their trips and make the same or similar statement: "I learned so much from the people of _[insert country]_." You'll learn things from local believers, missions staff and host families, things that you'll carry with you for years to come.

If both groups are learning one from the other you may wonder why "Shared Learning" is listed as a mistake. Simply put and all too frequently, time and opportunity is not given to STMers or nationals to do a combined debrief of sorts prior to participants heading home.

When you leave, you assume – at least you hope – that you've made even a small difference on the country you've been working in. If, however, you've avoided clustering, engaged in one-on-one conversations and one of those individuals specifically references something you taught them, you leave with concrete proof that you've made a difference. THAT feels good!

If that happens in a one-on-one conversation, imagine the compounded value of including nationals in a collective debrief at the end of your trip. The rewards are doubled: They have a chance to share what you and your team have taught them and reciprocally, you and your team have a chance to share what they've taught you.

If its powerful for you to hear, personally and specifically, how you have left something positive in the life and spirit of a national, imagine how powerful it would be for them to hear that they've impacted you spiritually as well.

There are times when group debriefs can't be organized for various reasons. If that's the case, simply make a point letting them know what they've taught you in an appropriate setting.

Shared learning happens, but we miss powerful opportunities for mutual encouragement and affirmation when time is not dedicated to verbalizing it.

3. New Forever-Friends?

Expectations can be tricky things.

You'll undoubtedly have high expectations of your STM involvement and that's normal. You'll be with like-minded, missions-minded individuals for a prolonged period of time. You'll spend morning, noon and night together – meaning that you'll get to know one another rather quickly. Together, you'll experience powerful services, times of deep worship and intense prayer, you'll overcome challenges and complete projects. Because of this, you and your teammates will "let the barriers down" so-to-speak, often sharing on a personal level.

More often than not this kind of exchange happens primarily with fellow team members but it's possible to experience this with members of the host team as well. Regardless, once a relationship has reached a certain level of depth, we can find ourselves expecting or assuming that we've just cemented a major, new relationship that will "last a lifetime."

My personal experience is that God uses some people to speak into our lives over the long-term and others for the short-term only. We tend to consider the long-term relationships as more valuable but that's not necessarily the case. Someone can come into our life for a short period of time but can be used of God to set us on a different direction than we'd have otherwise considered. Both types of relationships are valuable when they serve a God-ordained purpose in your life *(just as you can be serving a God-ordained purpose in theirs).*

Don't be overly concerned, during the trip, with qualifying which relationship will long-term and which might only be short term. That "filtering" happens naturally and is not always predictably. If and as opportunity allows, keep a door open to relationships; maintain them as possible and build on them when you're able. Social media makes this increasingly possible but only time will reveal which ones are truly long-term and which are short-term.

Let me end this section where I started, by saying that expectations can be tricky. Set your expectations too high ("We're going to be best friends forever") and you're poised for disappointment. Set them too low ("We'll probably just all go our separate ways afterward anyway… it's just the nature of short-term.") and you may miss out on some cool friendships. God placed these people in your life for a special reason at a specific time… because he wants you to be strength, encouragement and a blessing to each other; maybe now… maybe in the future.

4. I've just found my life's calling!

Consider the following train of thought which may cross your mind during, or soon after, your STM experience.

> "The past weeks have been an incredible time. I got out of my comfort zone, I've worked with great people, experienced deep things with the Lord and have seen very satisfying results. Perhaps this is what

God wants me to do for the rest of my life. This is IT… I'm coming back."

You begin to dedicate your energy and direct your efforts in that direction and start telling everyone your plans. "You're going back!"

Let me advise you to exercise caution. Making snap decisions and hasty open declarations *may* be a mistake. I say *"may"* be because I've seen it work both ways.

I made some hasty statements with regard to a projected return to Belgium. I did my 2-month term there in 1989 and felt called to return for a 2-year term which I successfully did from 1990-1992. It was a very positive time in my life. From 1992-1995, however, I was back in Canada finishing my B.A. and, to some extent, was mourning the absence of Belgium (in hindsight, partly due to a poor "post-missions re-entry") so I made plans to go back indefinitely. This time, the plans did not work out.

I've seen other people return from STM trips and make bold (and very public) statements within only weeks of their return. They were going back! It never materialized however and there was a sense of regret about the words spoken accompanied with confusion as to their ability to hear and recognize the voice of the Lord.

I get it. I really do. You've been away, experienced great things and felt personally validated because of your STM involvement. We all long to be part of something special and to enjoy the favor of our peers as a result, but those factors alone – those feeling – cannot replace the call of God with respect to your future plans. You don't want to plan a return if God is not in that plan.

What's more… it *could* be the plan and it *could* be the right place, but that doesn't mean that it's the right time. The heart is deceitful above all things so even though it may feel like the will of God at the time, only time will tell whether or not those feelings were just that… feelings, or whether they were the beginning of something more.

That begs the question, "How do you tell the difference?". The long version of this can be found in chapter three but here's the short version of how I handled a possible return to France after God spoke to me in 2012.

- o **Go slow!** Trying to rush things will be a great way to increase your frustration level… Guaranteed!
- o **Include a few trusted individuals** who know you well, who are spiritually sensitive and who can keep things hush-hush until you're ready to speak openly. *(hint: your pastor needs to be one of these people)*
- o **Pray, research and plan things out.** The more time you spend here, the better you'll be able to make an well-informed decision.

Let me remind you that in our case, I felt God's call in late August 2012, only spoke to 6 people in the ensuing months *(2 missionaries, 3 pastors and my wife)* and spent from November 2012 until January 2014 planning, before making any public statements. From then, we spent 12 more months preparing before we left North America in January 2015.

Slow and steady wins the race.
I highly recommend it!

5. Super-Hero Syndrome

We all have an ideal version of ourselves that we'd like to become and try to project. There can be an expectation that if we can just get to a place where no one knows us and we can make a fresh start, we'll have a better chance of becoming that ideal version of ourselves. We expect that our strengths will automatically come to the surface and our weaknesses fade to the background: We'll sing better, preach better, teach better, worship more freely and witness more boldly. We'll become a Super-Hero version of ourselves.

There's just one problem with that…
It doesn't work that way.

While a change of surrounding may offer you a fresh start, geography doesn't automatically make you a better version of you. If you tend to fly solo at home, don't expect to automatically be a great team player on the field. If you are really shy at home, then there's a good chance that solo-street ministry won't be your cup of tea on the field either. And if you lack confidence at home, you'll still struggle with that on the field as well.

When you pack your suitcase and prep your knapsack, those elements that make up your core personality will go with you… like it or not. You can, however, take comfort in the fact that just about everyone travelling with you will have the same "undeclared carry-on items" in their bags as well. Like you, they are aspiring to be the absolute best version of themselves.

In this manner, STM provides a bit of a greenhouse environment: creating ideal conditions for you to test out and potentially grow in new skills or new areas of involvement while still in a structured and closed environment. Still though, that "young plant" will have to come out of the greenhouse into a natural environment eventually. That's always a key moment in testing the vigor of the plant.

You can increase the chances of growth in new areas by doing one or two simple things:

o Be aware of your strengths and your weaknesses prior to leaving.

o If the Lord has put on your heart one or two specific areas where you'd like to see particular change (or at least have exposure to something new), talk about it with your pastor prior to leaving. Mention it to STM team leadership as well. As opportunities arise, they may be able to match you with situations where you can spread your wings a little.

Super-hero syndrome isn't as bad a thing as one might expect. It simply reflects a deeply held desire to become a better version of you. It doesn't happen automatically and requires work, but STM offers you a context in which it's possible to grow in new areas. Want to experience STM Success? Make a plan then work the plan... you can grow while away!

6. "I'll be a Better Christian after STM"

Those of us who have participated in, or organized, an STM endeavor would likely not have done so unless we believed this statement to be the case. We go because we desire to grow in some aspect of our personal Christian walk as well as our Christian service to the Lord. Surprisingly, however, there is a fair bit of evidence suggesting that long-term Christian growth isn't an automatic given as a result of STM. I won't go into it in great detail here (I've dedicated chapter eight to that) but let me give you an overview.

Several researchers interviewed STM participants prior to going, immediately after returning home and a year after their STM trip. For the sake of consistency, they generally focused on three areas: (a) participants' relationship with God (b) their relationship with the local church and (c) their relationship with the world.

What they typically found was that positive life change was most evident in the short-term (during the trip and shortly after returning home). Within a year, however, there was often little change over and above their "pre-trip" levels. This even included participants' giving to missions-related causes. Researchers' conclusions: the long-term effects of STM involvement are limited at best.

Part of me bristled at their conclusion because it was completely opposite to my experience. Still, I kept reading and found that they qualified their findings by indicating certain factors that are consistently present in the lives of those who *do* experience positive long-term change, namely:

- o People that take part in **multiple STM trips** have a greater chance of seeing those short-term changes "take hold" and lead to longer-term change.

- o The more a person invests in **pre-trip preparation** and structured **post-trip follow-up**, the greater the chance that positive long-term change will occur.

- o Participants whose **family and church family are highly supportive** of them stand a better chance of experiencing long term change than those participants who are somehow disconnected from the same.

You *can* be a better Christian as a result of one or several STM trips. It's not a given, but with planning, structure and accountability it is possible. You are considering STM because you want to grow as a Christian so make these three things a priority to boost your chances of long-term success.

7. Re-Entry? No Problem!

We're pretty good at relegating people and experiences to different "compartments" of our life. Sometimes there is cross-over but not always. Our colleagues from work, our church friends and our fellow students may not all be in the same circles. Similarly, our learning experiences can be compartmentalized as well… we learn "this" at school and apply it in a school context. We learn "that" at church and apply it there. We learn "these things" at work and that's where they stay.

So it can be when you return from STM. You may think that you can neatly just keep things that you learned and experienced while away, in the "STM box" and otherwise slip back into everyday life back home, with little difficulty.

Did you, or did you not, envision STM involvement as a way to shake things up a bit?

If you answered "yes" to that then please, fight against simply falling back into the norm. Strive for a new norm and as you do, know that there can be a few challenges along the way.

Re-entry issue #1: …Lack of understanding:

While you have been away, people back home have carried

on with their regular routines. All they know of your time away is what you've shared on social media or in personal communication. The deeply felt spiritual and social experiences that you've had are something that they can appreciate from a distance, but cannot share first-hand. Upon your return, they will show a genuine interest but don't be surprised if you find that interest waning after a while. It's not ill-intentioned, but since they didn't share that experience (particularly if they haven't had similar experiences in the past), they have a difficult time relating. If you see "the fog" descend on their expression, don't be upset, just hook up with one of your fellow STMers via social media and reminisce together.

Re-entry issue #2: ...You've changed!

You used to view things in your culture solely as a cultural insider. While you still *are* a cultural insider, you are now also are able to view, with another set of lenses, things that you never used to question. Let me give you an example: If your STM time has taken you to the developing world where even small things or limited resources are greatly valued, you may return home with a sense of injustice at what you now perceive as the "excesses" of North American life. It can be tough because you never saw it as problematic before yet you want your response to be balanced. If you want to adjust your own behavior in response to your new view by all means do so but be careful about projecting that on others. Remember, they haven't had the same experience. It's not impossible for you to influence behaviors around you but be humble and be wise if you try to do so.

Re-entry issue #3: ...Rose-Colored Glasses Syndrome

Because STM is generally a positive experience for participants (largely because it's a bit of a greenhouse environment) one temptation can be to idealize everything about the place, the culture and the people. Idealizing the "other" too much can lead you to become frustrated with – even criticize – your home environment.

> "The worship is more free."
> "The prayer is so fervent."
> "They're not concerned about time."
> ... said one STMer somewhere between the north and south poles!

One of the things that I have found helpful is to journal a my thoughts during times of change or readjustment. If you really stop to think about it, your time overseas was not without times of frustration or misunderstanding as well. Make an effort to also remember those times. Your home church is extraordinary at "this, this, this or this" ... write it down.

You've got to be realistic about both your home and your STM environments. Neither are perfect but both can be an enormous source of blessing if you take the best of both worlds and try to incorporate them into your life.

8. Connection to the Field

In our hyper-connected world it is extremely easy to be in contact and very natural to do so. You'll note that at various points in here, I've encouraged you to keep in touch with people connected to your STM endeavor, where that's possible, authentic and appropriate. Now I want to give you a caution with regard to keeping in touch.

Sometimes missions organizations have guidelines (or at least suggestions) around maintaining contact with people on the field. Trust that if there are guidelines, they're there for a reason and are generally a remedy for past-issues.

On one trip in particular, over the past thirty years, I exchanged info with folks while away (my mailing address as this was long before social media). For the most part I exchanged very normal letters with new friends there, but there came a time when I received a series of letters specifically requesting money be sent directly to a local church we'd been involved with. Had I been a pastor at the time, I could've chalked this up to a request for my church to help with a project, but I was an individual. It made for a few awkward exchanges.

While away, your heart-strings may well be plucked for a particular project and you may have it in your heart to do something, but if there is a local missionary on-site, I would always recommend funneling that money through established financial channels, designated to the project of your choice as opposed to sending it directly to individuals.

Summing Up

You embarked on your STM adventure with high hopes of real life change and positive experiences and I join you in hoping for the very best experience possible.

If you want to be assured of the very best, there are a few potential pitfalls that you should try to avoid. I've mentioned eight here and they are far from constituting an exhaustive list but if you are able to master these, then you are off to a great start in making sure that your time away is as much of a success as God and everyone around you is hoping it will be.

7

DISARMING FRUSTRATION

When planning for and looking forward to your STM experience, "frustration" is likely not one of the things you're preparing for, yet it *can* be part of your time away.

Below I indicate eight possible sources of frustration that can keep your time away from being as successful as you, and those around you, hope it will be.

1. The Application Process

To borrow a term from internet jargon, we are, without question a "fiber-op society" – we feel the need for speed. The application process however, can take months and when you're eagerly awaiting a response, it can feel more like you're on a dial-up connection rather than fiber-op.

Through the waiting process, missions staff or your pastor may bring you up to date from time to time or you may be left wondering, which can be a source of frustration. If you are of an analytical temperament, one of the consequences of this waiting game can be to question your calling, your abilities or even your ability to hear God's voice.

Relax and be patient. If God has called you, and you've

done all that you need to do to prepare… you'll get there. And you'll arrive at just the right time.

> *"He who began a good work in you*
> *is faithful to complete it."*
> Philippians 1:6

2. Team Dynamics

"You are going with 15 other young people and it's going to be fantastic!" … or perhaps "You'll be working alongside an incredible missionary, making you part of one of the most dynamic teams out there; Perfect!"

Teamwork undoubtedly creates opportunities for great growth, but if you only see them in terms of "fantastic" and "perfect" you may be setting yourself up for disappointment.

There will naturally be some level of affinity between you and those with whom you'll serve by virtue of the fact that you all have a heart for missions and for the country in which you're serving. Recognize, though, that it takes strong personalities to leave home and be involved in missions and sometimes strong personalities clash.

During my 1989, two-month term in Belgium I ended up clashing with one of my team-mates a couple of weeks in. I think it took us both by surprise and by the end of the two months the ship had more or less righted itself, but in the meantime it certainly affected us and no doubt affected the team as well.

Rough patches can happen with fellow team members or they can rise up between you and people on the ground. All it takes is for one person to be having a hard day and for the other to rub them the wrong way. Words can be exchanged and feelings hurt.

Not only is this just "life", but it can also be the enemy trying to plant division in the team. Being aware of the potential pitfall ahead of time, and taking steps to avoid it, can go a long way to reducing instances of frustration during your STM trip.

If something does arise, one of the most biblical things you can do (and one of the most effective for preserving a positive team dynamic) is to simply guard your tongue. Many proverbs talk about the wisdom of saying nothing, in addition to James' teaching on the power of the tongue. Do everything you can to preserve a strong team dynamic and not only will you be well appreciated by fellow team members but you'll definitely reduce your own frustration.

> *"…endeavouring to keep the unity of the Spirit*
> *in the bond of peace."*
> Ephesians 4:3

3. Language vs. Culture

In chapters three and four I talk about how linguistic ability can help you distill the will of God and potentially determine where you'll serve. I speak from experience however, when I tell you that knowing the language does not make you a cultural insider. The two are very different.

I have been an active French-learner since 1980, taught university-level French for eight years, have a Master's degree in French linguistics and have spent several years living in a French-language context. Still though, I have often felt like a cultural outsider.

There's a very good reason for that, I AM a cultural outsider. Language has given me a window into the culture and I may relate to it better than others, but I'm still on the outside looking in. French culture is not my culture. Faced with that, you have three options:

1. Deny your "otherness" and aspire to be "just like the _____" (insert the culture of your choice, in my case "French"). The problem is, you aren't just like them and constantly trying to be will only increase your frustration.

2. Don't even try to be like them and remain 100% North American. It is certainly the path of least resistance for you, but it could cause resistance among those of the culture you're trying to reach. Remember, you're a guest in their country and culture.

3. Realize that you can meet in the middle. Take the best aspects of your home culture, capitalize on that inherent difference and do your best to be all things to all men as Paul did.

   For example: As a North American, I'm less formal than the average Frenchman when it comes to personal interactions. The French social code calls for a great deal of formality, particularly in business settings. I've found that softening formality a bit (according to my nature), injecting a bit of Atlantic Canadian cheerfulness, and apologizing in advance (also VERY Canadian) for my lack of knowledge or for missteps, is very well received. They see that I'm willing to be a bit vulnerable and that prompts them to lower their "formality guard" as well.

In short remember, knowing the language doesn't make you a cultural insider in the short term and things can flow out of that which are cause for frustration. Recognizing that ahead of time will help you avoid being overly bound up when those situations do occur.

> *"I am made all things to all men,*
> *that I might, by all means, save some."*
> 1 Corinthians 9:22

4. "Tick Boxes"

When you decide to spend a prolonged time abroad, in more than simply a tourist capacity, you sacrifice yet another easily taken for granted luxury, being able to tick boxes easily.

Tick boxes are everywhere; on job applications, medical forms, income tax documents, sports club materials, even online forms. When you lead a "normal" life… it's easy to tick off the boxes.

- ☑ Full-Time Employee
- ☑ Resident of (state/province)
- ☑ Eligible for Family Allowance
- ☑ Contributing to 401K / RRSP

When you spend a significant amount of time on the mission field as an STMer however, the boxes aren't as easily ticked and you have to constantly explain:

- ☐ **Employment status:** "I'm not officially an employee but I do receive a regular income from the missions sending organization."

- ☐ **Residency:** My physical residence is France but

I'm technically a tax-resident of Canada even though my income-provider *(not employer)* is located in the United States. (That's always a fun one. All they can do is just shake their head and smile, silently expressing "I don't really get it but I'm just glad it's you and not me!")

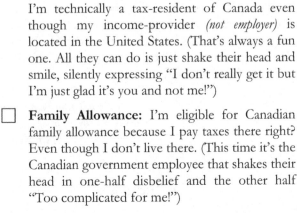 **Family Allowance:** I'm eligible for Canadian family allowance because I pay taxes there right? Even though I don't live there. (This time it's the Canadian government employee that shakes their head in one-half disbelief and the other half "Too complicated for me!")

Retirement Planning: Already placed contributions can remain in place, but new ones cannot be initiated... maybe? If you stay out of the country too long... then what!? Not everyone will give you the same answer, not even within the same government office.

When you make the decision to spend a prolonged amount of time out of the country (depending on your stage of life) it can mean a lot more bureaucracy to sort through.

When I spent two years in Belgium as a single man between the ages of twenty and twenty-two, there were much fewer things to take into consideration. I returned to Canada and moved back into my parents' basement. As a husband and father of three however, considerations have multiplied. The tick boxes cannot be ticked quite so easily anymore and that can be frustrating. Take it in stride, remain patient, work diligently and trust the Lord.

5. Adulting in the 21st Century

Our society places a great deal of emphasis on certain

marks of adulthood and stability. These can include things like retirement planning as I mentioned above, but it can also involve things like home ownership, educational funds for kids (if you have children) and the "stability" that comes with a regular job.

Following God's call to missions involvement flies in the face of stability as the world defines it. That thought can weigh heavily on your mind whether you serve as a single person or have a family in tow.

What's more, your future – as a missionary – depends on a combination of:

o The continued call of God (which can evolve)
o Continued open doors in your country of service (which can change) and
o Financial support from churches and individuals (some of whom may or may not be able to fulfill their financial commitment for a variety of reasons).

In essence, your future is subject to change and change is the opposite of stability.

If you're an STMer considering longer-term missions involvement, you are especially vulnerable. You may or may not be sure how God is directing or what the timeline is. Spiritually speaking, we know that our stability comes from being in the Lord's will, but in the physical realm, the lack of certainty can be at best, a test of faith and at worst, frustrating.

Make no mistake, you need to do everything possible to ensure that you are "adulting" appropriately. As much as possible, you need to be making plans for the future but beyond what you are able to plan for, know that we can say, like Paul said to Timothy:

> *"I know whom I have believed,*
> *and am persuaded that His is able*
> *to keep that which I've committed*
> *unto Him against that day."*
> 2 Timothy 1:12

In other words… do what you can to "adult" appropriately and leave the rest in God's capable hands.

6. Fundraising

It's not uncommon for missionaries, be they short-term or long-term, to want to get to the field of their calling and to arrive… Yesterday! So the prospect of spending months, or even years, fund-raising before being able to go can be a source of frustration. You can find yourself constantly thinking "If only I were there already, great things would be happening" or "Maybe I'm missing out by not being there yet." You need to be careful that the waiting period doesn't cast a negative shadow over your time of preparation; a time when you should be preparing yourself to minister, gaining experience, investing through prayer.

Let me offer you two words of wisdom with regard to fundraising or "deputation".

Word of Wisdom #1

A wise missionary friend once told me this: "You can't separate ministry "on the field" from deputation (ministry "off the field"). You have to see deputation as part of your overall ministry, otherwise it will frustrate you."

Although my role as a relatively long-term short-termer has not yet required me to do a multi-year deputation, I can see how that would be so.

What I *can* offer up from my own experience is this…

Word of Wisdom #2

From the time we announced (Jan. 2014) our AIM departure to France and actually landing onsite (Jan. 2015) we "waited" roughly 53 weeks. I say waited, but that waiting involved extensive travel through the Atlantic District, and a handful of services elsewhere, on weekends while still working full time during the week. This is how we raised a portion of our monthly financial commitments.

More than just financial commitments however, we also gained a deeper sense of connection with fellow ministry families and churches in our area. It goes without saying that you see people at functions or across aisles, but something special happens when those same ministers take you into their home for a meal or share dinner at a local restaurant. Words of encouragement, inspiration and prophecy were spoken across dining room tables.

Our "waiting time" was more than just fundraising, it was a time for carving out an even deeper connection with the family of God that also just happened to make up a good portion of our financial base.

The way you look at fundraising will have a profound effect on whether it's a source or frustration or a time of great value. Look for the value.

7. Financial Limitations on the Field

When you are home, living your "normal" (non-missions) life, you may not think about finances as much as you will while away on missions.

- o Friends going out for dinner after church? You don't even think about it... you're going too.

- o Need a new pair of runners for your morning jog? Just dig out your credit card.

- o No-name vs. brand name? Hands-down, you reach for the brand-name.

At home you're either still living at home or you're working full-time. You know month-to-month what you can expect to come in and your credit card is always an option. While on missions however, that assurance is not there to the same degree.

- o Financial support can vary from month to month.

- o Fluctuating exchange rates can affect the value of what does come in monthly.

- o Some financial partners may be unable to continue their support, or continue at the same level.

You may have to forego the restaurant meals more often than you would at home. You may need to be more strategic about what would otherwise be straight-forward purchases. In the long-term, it's a very good learning experience, but a decreased lack of financial freedom can be a source of frustration.

Recognize though that these limitations are likely just for a time and that it represents an opportunity for personal growth. Many a senior, fully funded missionary began their missions involvement at a much lower level of funding. Through patience and faithfulness in the lean times, they were rewarded with spiritual fruit and as time went on, news of their faithfulness having spread, saw finances flow in as well.

If your STM is scheduled to last a couple of weeks, this may be less of a frustration for you for the end is in sight from the beginning. If your trip will see you gone for a couple of months, this will similarly be of limited consequence for you. The longer your stay on the field, the more the temptation of this frustration may come knocking at your door. A key to combating it?

"I have learned, in whatsoever state I am,
therewith to be content."
Philippians 4:11

8. Frustration through Comparison

Social networking has given STMers many advantages in terms of regular communication with family back home and with supporters near and far. But it comes with a potential disadvantage as well – comparison.

Imagine, if you will: You have been working for two months in a given field, quietly going about the work that you have been entrusted with. On the surface, there appears to be little change or growth. Then you log on to Facebook or Twitter over a cup of coffee in your down time, and here's what you see:

- o **Missionary A** in country X shares a photo of 6 baptismal candidates still dripping wet.

- o **Missionary B** in country Y reports of 10 receiving the baptism of the Holy Ghost.

o **Missionary C** in country Z has a video of their newest daughter work with 87 in attendance.

If your assignment is not one that's given to clear measurables, and if your tenure is long enough (with few measurables), then you could easily find yourself given to feelings of inadequacy or ineffectiveness. Unintentionally, you begin to compare yourself, and your contribution to missions, with missionaries A, B & C.

There are several problems with such comparison:

1. **Location:** Generally speaking, people's response in Europe and the Middle East will be quite different from those in Latin America, Africa and some parts of Southeast Asia. To judge your effectiveness based on people's response elsewhere is to do yourself a great disservice.

2. **Capacity:** If your job description is teaching in a Bible School or doing administrative support for missions staff then once again, measuring your effectiveness by baptisms, Holy Ghost infillings or by church growth will be problematic. You will no doubt take great joy in seeing those things occur in your setting when they do, but they are not your primary measure of effectiveness.

3. **Personal Expectations:** What are (were) your personal expectations prior to going? Are they appropriate? Are they based on collaborative discussion with mission staff or established in a silo? These expectations will go a long way to encouraging a sense of satisfaction or dissatisfaction during your time away. Discuss expectations with your pastor prior to leaving. Do you feel your expectation is the result of

something God put in your spirit, again, discuss it with your pastor, the missionary or mission staff. Appropriately set expectations will go a long way in helping your STM experience be positive.

4. **Job Description:** This is closely tied to the question of expectations although it is primarily an expression of the expectations of the sending organization or the receiving missionaries with whom you'll be working. If you don't have one you can't be sure that you're meeting *their* expectations and that can lead you to second-guess your effectiveness.

5. **Time on Field:** If your STM term is only a matter of a couple of weeks or months, the element of comparison will be less present. Shorter trips tend to be highly structured with more defined measurables. This isn't to say that there are *fewer* expectations, or that comparison is *absent*, simply the expectations are different and comparison is relatively short-lived. The longer you spend on the field the more you may deal with comparison as a source of frustration.

While comparison, during your STM term, is problematic for the reasons cited above (among other reasons I'm sure), perhaps the greatest reason to consciously avoid comparison is that it's just not Biblical.

> *"So then neither is he that planteth any thing, neither he that watereth; but God that giveth the increase… every man shall receive his own reward* **according to his own labour**. *For we are labourers together with God."*
> 1 Corinthians 3:7-9

*"For we dare not… compare ourselves with some that commend themselves: but they… comparing themselves among themselves, **are not wise**."*
2 Corinthians 10:12

*We are "stewards of the mysteries of God. Moreover it is required in stewards, that a man be found **faithful**."*
1 Corinthians 4:2

Comparison is almost unavoidable, given our human nature, and those feelings will likely find root in the mind of everyone involved in Christian ministry at one point or another. If you happen to find yourself experiencing such feelings, the double-edged sword of social media has the potential to amplify such feelings. While the danger of comparison is by no means limited to service on the mission field, I do think that the potential for comparison can be amplified when serving abroad.

In preparation for your time away, pray that God make these verses from Paul's letters to the Corinthians come alive to you. You are a laborer **with** God and will receive your own reward according to your own labor.

So labor well. Your success is not determined by the swell of social media but by your faithfulness to do the work that God has called and equipped you to do.

The Danger of Frustration

Like with many things, the presence of frustration in our lives doesn't mean that we've missed God's call, it doesn't necessarily mean that God has lifted His call and it doesn't mean that our gifts, talents and abilities are not being used. The presence of frustration simply means that there's a "kink in the hose" … something that needs to be straightened out.

Problems arise when the frustration is prolonged, when it ceases to occupy a reasonable place in our experience and begins to take center stage; increasingly dominating our thoughts and eventually getting voiced or impacting our actions. At this point it becomes a long-term stressor and is out of balance.

When prolonged and out of balance, though we can be in the will of God, frustration will make us question whether or not we truly are. We can have heard from God, but frustration will bring that into question. We lose confidence in ourselves, our ability to hear from God or to trust His ability to see us through.

Properly balanced, frustration can be a useful impetus, pushing us to make positive change that will result in greater effectiveness.

Don't let frustration get the best of you. Strive to take every thought captive to the obedience of Christ (2 Corinthians 10.5) and involve one or two trusted mentors or prayer warriors. Don't try to fight frustration alone... it's always more difficult.

Summing it Up

Because we're planning to involve ourselves in the work of the Kingdom, we can sometimes start with the idea that all will go smoothly and everything will just "work out". While I agree that things do generally "work out", the very fact that we use that term means that something isn't currently working or going as we'd expected or hoped. We've run into an obstacle and perhaps we're experiencing frustration.

If, on the other hand, you expect some element of frustration and you prepare yourself for it, you equip yourself to manage the frustration rather than having it get the best of you. It would be a shame for momentary (or prolonged) frustration to rob you of some of the joy associated with serving the Lord in missions.

8

REVERSE CULTURE SHOCK

Allow me to dedicate a few pages to the importance of follow-up; helping the STMer navigate the waters of reverse culture shock.

First of all we need to recognize that the degree to which re-entry back to the home culture will mainly depend on two factors: (a) the length of time spent abroad and (b) the degree to which their STM culture differed from their home culture.

It goes without saying that STMers who are away for a year or more will experience more reverse culture shock than someone who takes part in a 2-week trip. That being said, someone who spends two weeks in Europe will likely experience less culture shock than someone who spends two weeks in Central America or Africa.

Tips and strategies to help minimize reverse culture shock are provided in various parts of this book, as well as in the Appendix, but let me underscore why it's important to proactively manage re-entry.

My Own Re-Entry Gone Bad

I briefly detailed my own re-entry story in chapter two, but let me refresh your memory and fill in a few blanks. I spent two years (1990-1992) as a Canadian Baptist Volunteer in Belgium (a French speaking country in western Europe) without coming home. The missionary leadership team was comprised of one Canadian family and one Belgian missionary family. Our immediate neighborhood was heavily influenced by Sicilian culture and the two established churches we worked most closely with were of Belgo-Italian and Polish cultures. It all made for quite a mixture really.

After those two years, I returned home with plans to complete my Bachelor's degree at a secular university, having attended a Christian liberal arts college between high school and going to Belgium. Until 1992, I was almost constantly surrounded by a very structured Christian culture and peer group. That changed when I returned home from Belgium.

Key Friendships

I was strong in my faith and involved in my local church, but my immediate peer group had changed dramatically during my time away. The core of our youth group had moved on to different stages of life (some were away for university, some had married and some were now in the workplace full time) and those key relationships now had an unintended but very real gap in them. Youthful idealism assumes that friendship doesn't change over time, but age and experience knows that that's not the case. Friendships *do* change and mine had. That caught me by surprise.

Pastoral Leadership

The other major change that happened during my absence was a change in pastoral leadership at my church. I had never met the new pastor prior to coming home and there was no relationship there to speak of; not intentional of course, it was simply just a matter of fact.

The sum total of both of those changes was this: the support network that I so badly needed to help me navigate re-entry was left severely compromised. This at a time where, for the first time in my young-adult life, I was primarily surrounded by predominantly secular student culture. What's more, few and far between were instances where I could connect with people who bridged both worlds; my home life and my life on the field.

I mentioned in chapter two that I began to drift during that time. God spared me from things that would bear long-term consequences, but I was drifting nonetheless.

At these times I needed someone that embodied two elements:

(a) someone with whom I had a relationship of trust and to whom I could say: "The former missions volunteer that everyone thinks is doing great, isn't actually doing so well and needs help." *and*

(b) someone whose walk with God inspired me deeply, enough to help me pull myself up by the bootstraps.

I was slowly starving and it wasn't immediately visible. I might've looked alright on the outside, but spiritually I was emaciated.

The same thing happened to a friend of mine who spend a year abroad. They were unable to fully "find their place" upon returning home. Their life took a number of turns for which scars will be long-lasting.

113

Re-entry is important.

Though I didn't have long-term consequences like my friend, the frustration I was facing did lead me to a point where I left the church in which I'd spent the first twenty-five years of my life and eventually led me to my own personal Pentecost. I don't regret the trajectory that brought me into Pentecost, neither do I belittle my heritage. I highlight my experience for one reason only, to repeat that re-entry (how we handle reverse culture shock) is very, very important.

It Takes a Team

Properly managing re-entry is not the sole responsibility of the STMer. Depending on their age and or life experience, they may be totally ill-equipped to emotionally process re-entry on their own. For this reason there are three other individuals or groups that make up the support team necessary to facilitate transition back to everyday life.

Sending organizations are in the business of STM and for this reason they play (or should play) a central role in facilitating re-entry. They see participants involved in various fields across the globe and while the details of reverse culture-shock may vary from field to field, the overarching themes are similar. While they're "experts" in managing re-entry however, due to distance they will not have regular contact with participants. Their expertise (unless very structured) will be only part of the solution.

Local pastors play a vital role because they act as a bridge between participants and sending organizations. They are (we hope) very involved in the application process, and a key part of the support network while on the field. What's more, they are a key spiritual voice in the life of that participant. Ideally, they have a strong relationship with the STMer and are able to speak into their life, be it for edification, encouragement, teaching or correction. While local pastors have regular contact however, they also have many things vying for their attention. Also, they don't possess the same level of expertise as the sending organization in terms of common re-entry issues.

Local church members and **key supporters** make up the third part of this team. When STM participants return from the field, there will be times when they need a listening ear. At other times, they may experience frustration because they've seen different methods produce results, methods which may be different from how things are done at home. As a group, you have the benefit of approachability. You'll be working alongside the STMer on a day-to-day basis and you are trusted peers. Your disadvantage, however, is that like the pastor, you don't possess the expertise that sending organization staff possess. Nor do you necessarily possess the ministerial experience and insight that a pastor has.

You see that each of these three groups has a vital role to play and each one in isolation is insufficient to help STMers successfully navigate the waters of re-entry.

I my case, local church members were a very good support network, but the key element of trusted and open communication with pastoral leadership was missing. It eventually became enough of an issue that I was prepared to walk away from the only home church I'd known for the first twenty-five years of my life.

Pastors, churches, missionary organizations: Re-entry is important. You've invested too much in young people to see them lose out as a result of mismanaged re-entry. We need to find a streamlined way for all three of these key players to work together. If there is a lot to potentially lose, there is also a lot to gain by a well-managed re-entry.

STMer: If people around you seem unable to relate to your time away, it's not intentional. Just as you might be unable to understand how they "don't get it" or "aren't able to understand or appreciate your experience" they may not understand why you don't just slide back into your home culture as if nothing changed.

When you're having a tough time dealing with reverse culture shock, find someone to talk to. If your pastor is available, seek him out. If one of your peers is available, seek them out. If your best friend is available, seek them out. If a fellow STM participant is also local and is available, grab a coffee together and talk.

One of the advantages that you have today that I did not have between 1992 and 1995 is interaction via the web. Social media gives you the advantage of easy contact with other STM team-members alongside whom you served. If you're having re-entry woes, they probably are as well. If anybody can relate to what you're feeling, they can.

Both you and they likely have similar feelings of having left your heart in another country even as your body climbed back on the flight home. Some of the best "therapy" that you can get by times is just talking to someone else who truly "gets it."

So make use of electronic tools and personal meet-ups to help you navigate re-entry. Transitioning well back to your home culture won't happen automatically, it takes intentional management. Others can help you but others don't always know when you're most in need of their help so again, reach out.

Section 2

STM
Research & Recommendations

9

LONG-TERM CHANGE
...OR NOT?

Several assumptions are commonly made about the long-term impact of STM involvement and these expected benefits are placed front and center when promoting opportunities. The short version sounds like this:

"Eyes will be opened, hearts will be transformed and lives will be changed forever."[3]

STMers impact the places to which they travel and the people with whom they work, but time away will be of personal benefit as well. That three-pronged expectation is one reason that pastors and churches support STMers and STM endeavors. Pastors also invest because they expect or hope (and rightfully so) that participants will return to the local church "on fire" and more equipped to be involved in the work locally.

Above, I gave the short-version of what is expected of STM. The long version would look a bit more like this.

---

[3] **VerBeek, Kurt Alan** *(2008)*, "Lessons from the Sapling: Review of Quantitative Research on Short-Term Missions.

You can expect STM participants to manifest, in the long run, some of the following:

- Increased church involvement
- Greater Christian maturity and service
- Increased missions giving (once in the workforce)
- Future missions interest or involvement
- Greater awareness of their abilities & limitations
- Increased sense of God's limitless abilities

I've seen pretty much all of those things manifest themselves in my life as a result of long-term STM involvement. Because of my experience, I would be the first to espouse them and promote them in turn. But if I were to believe some STM research, I'd have to consider myself the exception, not the rule.

In this chapter I'm going to highlight and comment on excerpts and ideas from the following researchers who have studied STM *(full bibliographical references in Appendix)*.

- **Friesen, Randall Gary** *(2004)*, "Improving the Long-Term Impact of Short-Term Missions",

- **Taylor, William Vaughan** *(2012)*, "Short-Term Missions: Reinforcing Beliefs and Legitimizing Poverty"

- **VerBeek, Kurt Alan** *(2006)*, "The Impact of Short-Term Missions – A Case Study of House Construction in Honduras after Hurricane Mitch".

- **VerBeek, Kurt Alan** *(2008)*, "Lessons from the Sapling: Review of Quantitative Research on Short-Term Missions.

Summary of their Research

VerBeek (2006) surveyed 162 STM participants who traveled to Honduras to rebuild houses after 1998's hurricane Mitch. His research suggested that the "STM trips had resulted in very little lasting positive change in either the lives of the North Americans or the Hondurans" (VerBeek, 2008, p.3). His 2008 study was an attempt to see whether the 2006 study was an exception or was supported by broader research. What he found was that "eleven of the thirteen studies [he researched] found little or no significant positive impact from the STM trip in the lives of participants [over the long term]." (ibid.)

Friesen (2004) looked at variables, associated with STM experiences, that would affect participants' relationship with God, the church and the world in general. He found that,

> "While the positive impact of the short-term mission experience was significant, the post-trip regression in participants' beliefs, attitudes and behaviors one year after returning from the mission experience was also significant." (Friesen, 2004, p.iii)

Taylor (2012), for his part, took part in a 1996 STM trip to Honduras, subsequently returned for a longer period and led multiple trips to Central America. "Many people said the trips changed their life, but it was never clear what exactly had changed." (Taylor, 2012, p.2) In his Master's thesis, he interviewed twenty people who had taken part in Christian-based STM projects and focused on their relationship to and discourse on poverty and the poor. One of his conclusions:

> "Short-term missions did not radically

transform participants. Instead, the change is a slight amplification of existing beliefs that reinforce the status quo." (Taylor, 2012, p.iv)

While this book isn't intended to be academic in nature, it is good to periodically get outside of one's day-to-day context, if only to be able to look back on it with a fresh set of eyes.

These articles speak about STM in a broad sense and are not limited to one or another Christian denomination. If you enjoy academic reading, I recommend the full articles to your attention. If you're just looking for the top level detail, no worries, that's what I want to give you here.

I'm not trying to discourage you, honest!

It may seem as though, by presenting the findings of these researchers at the end of the book, I'm trying to undermine any progress I may have made in convincing you to get (even further) on board with STM. That's not the case.

My hope is that by presenting some of their conclusions about what *can* happen, you will be able to avoid common pitfalls and make *your* experience a resounding success.

Let's begin.

Some Numbers

If you're interested in STM, you're not alone. In fact the trend has grown exponentially, particularly among North American Christians. VerBeek (2006) says that in 1989 there were roughly 125,000 people who participated in STM opportunities but that by 2003, that number had grown well beyond 1 million. Friesen (2004) states that between 1998 and 2001 alone, there was a 256% increase in the number of people taking STM trips. That's a lot of people!

VerBeek (2008) extrapolates saying that if an estimated 1,5 million people are taking STM trips each year, it's not unreasonable to expect that the dollar figure associated with all those people and all that travel be figured in the billions of dollars. That's a lot of money!

What makes so many people want to give up time and spend money to take part in STM? And what drives so many others to fund and send them?

What drives STM participation?

STM supporters would say that it represents an expression of the individual's desire to be part of fulfilling the great commission. Critics of STM (yes, there are critics) reduce it to little more than Christian group travel. My experience makes me describe STM as something more middle-of-the-road: it comprises both of those motivations and more.

There are at least three things driving the upsurge in STM participation.

1. Ease of Travel

The first thing driving ever-increasing participation is the ease with which people can travel further and further abroad at an increasingly reasonable cost. Perhaps an unintentional side-effect of globalization. The short duration of many STM opportunities along with the fact that it's accessible to young people, retirees and everyone in between also contributes to high participation rates.

MIKE LONG

Historically, missions involvement meant committing years of one's life, if not an entire lifetime. You had to really, *really* be sure the Lord was calling you to missions because trial runs just didn't exist. Today, people trying to determine whether or not God is calling them to long-term missions involvement have many chances to get their feet wet before taking the proverbial plunge.

Coming out of the research however, two other factors seem to consistently contribute to the exponential grown in STM participation since the 1990s.

Pastors and participants alike take note.

2. Participants are looking for purpose.
They want to change and grow

...and as we've seen, they are willing to invest a great deal of time, energy and finances in order to do so.

VerBeek noted the North Americans' reaction to Hondurans and how happy they always appear; STMers admire and even idealize that happiness. He suggests, however, that such a response "may also reveal how discontented North Americans are despite [their] material wealth." (VerBeek, 2006, p.491). Taylor (2012), for his part, points to "missions high" or "mountain top experiences", a desire for intense spiritual fulfillment (p. 8) as a factor driving missions participation.

(a) Purpose

Is it possible that the upswing in STM participation over the past thirty years is related, albeit indirectly, to an overall increase in disposable personal income and an increasing abundance of "stuff"? Is it possible that we North Americans almost feel trapped by our consumer lifestyle? Is it possible that deep down we are wanting to connect to and be part of something more purposeful? Is it possible that even our traditional (in some cases almost institutionalized) Christian culture is periodically lacking in that sought-after depth and connection?

If so, STM provides a great outlet for young people to be part of change and growth, particularly in the short term. It's easier to embrace change when separated from our day-to-day life.

While Christian mission trips used to be the mainstay of these cross-cultural endeavors we no longer have the monopoly on meaningful times of service. There are many choices for people who would like to do something meaningful abroad, and many of them completely divorced from God. People can go abroad to teach English, help with sustainable development, literacy and education projects, and the like. It's not that those projects are without value, but without being connected to the gospel they are devoid of *eternal* value.

Pastor, if people from your church, "have the itch" to do something meaningful, help them find an outlet. Don't settle, or let them settle, for something that's disconnected from the gospel or something that's being organized by a secular organization. Help them find *their* purpose by being involved in *His* purpose.

(b) Change & Growth

Sure, change and growth can be initiated just about anywhere at anytime, given the right circumstances. The nature of the resulting growth will be determined by the predominant influences (or influencers) involved.

A common thread ran through the excerpts I included above from the three researchers: Definite change in the lives of participants, was observable and measurable both during and immediately following their trips.

Change and growth are possible!

Why shouldn't it be? After all, participants have removed themselves from the day-to-day distractions that compete for attention and energy that God wants to see directed at Him and His purposes. Of course He will reveal Himself to and initiate growth in these STMers.

The trick is taking those changes, and that growth, that are occurring in the short term, and encouraging their continuation in the long term.

Think about the law of inertia for a moment. It states that more energy is required to *get* a body in motion that is currently at rest, than it does to *keep* a moving body *in* motion. Apply that to STM and what you have is this:

> *God, together with STM organizers, do the hardest part while participants are away… initiating change and growth in their life… getting things moving so to speak.*

In order for an STM experience to be considered successful in the long-term, that positive change and growth initiated on the mission field, needs to be brought back into participants' North American life.

That's where the STMers home church and sending pastor's roles become vital. More on that next chapter.

3. Participants want meaningful social connections.

Finally, the third thing that participants are looking for, when they take part in STM is new opportunities for meaningful social connections.

Taylor (2012) states that STM trips "strengthen intra-group bonds" (p.8). He goes so far as to say that much of the focus of STMers is on themselves, rather than on the places or the people that they visit. (p.116).

It's valuable to remember that there are two social connections possible in STM: connection with hosts in the receiving country and connection with intra-organizational team-members (whether host missionaries, in the case of solo STM service or with other team members in the case of group travel).

(a) Same-Culture Connection

It goes without question that bonding will occur more quickly and easily with people from our own language and culture. I mentioned some of the expectations and benefits around this in chapters six and seven and will underscore their importance one more time in the next chapter. For now though, drawing from my own experience, here is one of the ways in which participants can benefit greatly from STM team friendships.

STM participants go through a unique experience together. They experience powerful emotions and work together under a great many circumstances. Those ingredients combine to forge powerful connections. Other participants have seen you, to some degree, at your best – heavily dependant on the Lord for strength, seeking and serving him for all you're worth. In essence, they connect with the very best "version" of you. For this reason, they are uniquely placed to speak to you on that level further down the road; perhaps to help draw the best out of you at a later date, when that might be necessary and when it feels like no one else can relate to what you're feeling.

You will be able to laugh and share memories with many of your team members down the road and those times are necessary. Sometimes an hour or two spent reminiscing is good therapy. With some, however, the connection will be deep enough that you'll be able to share more – and there will be times when you'll need that too. These are the long-term connections that I spoke of in chapter 6. If you keep your heart and spirit open to them, they may be able to speak into you when few others can.

(b) Cross-Culture Bonding

Forging meaningful connections with people from your host culture is different but can be every bit as valuable and enriching. In all likelihood, the connections will be less frequent and may take a bit more effort at first, particularly if language comes into play, but God can use them to fulfill a purpose in your life as well. It could be in seemingly simple ways, for example the way some cultures ask more direct questions than North Americans do. God could use that to make you question your actions or attitudes in a particular area. It could be the way they exercise their faith that God will bring back to your memory when your own faith seems low. Perhaps the purpose will only reveal itself over time, maybe even years later.

There was a young man that I met southern France in 1996, while touring with the Continental Singers. He was young in his service to the Lord but faithful and open. We corresponded periodically over the years; sometimes yearly and other times we'd go 2-3 years without being in touch.

Very often though something in his letters would be an encouragement to me or would challenge me in some way. In March of 2017 we were able to reconnect for the first time in twenty-one years. We spent a day together and God used him, once again, to speak into my life.

Time and again I've experienced that odd sensation where, though I'd left home to minister to someone in a different place, God has used someone in that different place to minister to me.

STM participants want to make strong and meaningful social connections and what better context in which to connect to new people than with a group of committed fellow believers with a heart to serve the Lord.

I appreciate that the research gives insight into what motivates STMers into action – over and above the great commission. There is, however, a "flip side of the coin"; one that troubles me.

The Down Side

A common theme among the four researchers is the relatively short life-span of any positive change or growth association with STM work. While there was a general *increase* in life-change metrics during the STM term, that positive personal change often did not extend to the long-term and was often almost non-existent within a year of returning home.

In my mind, this represents the biggest learning opportunity to come out of the research.

Friesen's work is the research most focused on measuring lasting positive change in the lives of STM participants.

Respondents provided feedback on 24 behaviors and beliefs that impacted or reflected their relationship with God, with the local church and the world in general. Some of those 24 are listed below in the three major categories:

Relationship with God: prayer, worship, the Bible as a guide for life, stewardship of time and finances, purity, etc.

Relationship with the church: relationship with and service in the local church, teamwork in ministry, experience of spiritual authority, etc.

Relationship with the world: evangelism, compassion for human need, respect for cultures & values, value of social justice, etc.

Friesen sought their feedback prior to leaving, upon return and in a third session, one year later. The third assessment is, in my mind, of great importance because it captures participants' feedback after the initial rush of the "mountaintop" was past and allows measurement of any long-term change.

Generally, he found that 20 of the 24 metrics increased during STMers' time away but subsequently decreased within the following year, in some cases even going below pre-trip levels. **Positive short-term change was followed with regression in the long term.**

The Goal = Change

Let's be clear. Yes, organizers and sending churches desire to see participants make a difference while on the field; to see them involved in the work of the great commission. That goes without saying. But given the cost involved in sending individuals or teams abroad, if "impact on the field" was the *only* concern, why not simply send funds to the field and get more "bang for your buck"? VerBeek, 2006 (pp.482-3) deals with this question and relays the comment from recipients of STM ministry that "If they come, they should come for the friendships, for the cultural exchange... the most important is the relationship with the people." He also says that participants "left changed, not because someone told them about the work, but because they came and saw it for themselves." (ibid.)

The fact that we send people, not just money, shows that we want to see lives changed, not just on the field but those of participants as well.

Taylor indicates that while we talk about change, the "life-changing quality" is actually difficult to pin down. If you ask people *how* STM changed their life, they have a hard time giving specifics off the cuff. Yet his research indicates that STM experiences "reinforce existing beliefs. ...They are symbolically significant events that serve as makers ...and reflect how they see themselves. (Taylor, p.106) He further nuances the connection by saying that STM can amplify existing beliefs (ibid.p.113) later in his paper.

STM helps our young people and church members to see and define themselves apart from their secular or day-to-day occupations. The question still remains though... how do we encourage lasting positive change?

Friesen offers up the following specific observations that can help us. Here are some of the key findings that come out of his research.

Various Factors and
their Relationship to Change

(Friesen 2004, pp.6-9)

1. Participants with extensive **pre-trip discipleship training** had higher change scores during assignment in beliefs, attitudes and behaviors relating to:

   o Prayer
   o Bible as a guide to life
   o Value of Christian community
   o Relationship with the local church
   o Evangelism"

2. **The longer the STM experience**, the deeper and more lasting the impact on beliefs, attitudes and behaviors.

3. **STMers who serve as part of a team** will grow in terms of how they value Christian community.

4. **First timer STMers** will experience the broadest overall change while away, but will also show the greatest regression within the following year.

5. **Strong and supportive families** cultivate relational skills that can help participants solidify long term change.

6. The **strong support of home churches** can be interpreted as interest in the individual's overall personal development... which extends to the long-term.

7. Participants in **Relationship-focused projects** have better change-retention than those who participated in primarily service based projects.

8. **STMers who have done several trips** are

typically better able to retain the positive changes cultivated while away.

If one of the goals of STM is to see long term change in the lives of participants, then Friesen's observations give us a bit of a roadmap to ensuring that such growth takes place: That STMers experience success in the long-term.

I'll develop those factors in the next chapter where I offer up recommendations for pastors, participants and home churches; recommendations that will help these three groups work together to help ensure long-term positive change.

10

RECOMMENDATIONS

This chapter is based on a combination of my own experience as well as research presented in the previous chapter. The intent is slightly different for the three potential audiences

Audience #1:
STM Participants

STMers, here's what you need to look for in the following recommendations. Look for ways that you can plan to be really in tune with the people and tasks associated with your trip. Not only will it allow you to be more effective on the field, it will also help ensure that true long-term growth occurs in your own life.

1. **Plan your Plan:** As soon as you find out that your application has been accepted, get yourself a journal and begin writing things down as they relate to your trip.

   o If God has given you dreams or promises regarding the trip… record them.

   o If you have personal goals… record them.

- o If people have spoken words of prophecy about it... record them.

- o If you have fears you'd like to overcome... record them.

Writing them down will give you a starting point for your plan: what you'd like to achieve during your time away.

Your plan should be designed to help you navigate your time away as well as your transition back home. You will benefit greatly from your pastor's leadership and the experience of the sending organization, but it is first and foremost up to you to ensure that you are on top of details that lie within your control.

Don't neglect the spiritual side of preparation as well.

- o Orient a specific part of your prayer life around your time away.

- o Read books about missionaries. This can help open your eyes to spiritual challenges that are faced on the mission field but can also help increase your faith.

- o Speak to retired missionaries or former STMers around you. Pick their brain and glean from them.

2. **Plan your Trip:** Your pastor will already be aware of your application but once you've recorded some of your "Plan the Plan" items, discuss them with him. Making yourself accountable to him will increase your chances of meeting any personal goals you set.

   Plan the timeline with him in terms of financing, scheduling services (in-house or outside) and "working the plan".

Ask him for any recommended reading suggestions concerning your goals or any discipleship material that he'd like to see you go through in preparation.

3. **Plan your Return:** This is perhaps the most overlooked step but is just as important as the trip itself if you are to truly experience positive long-term change. Here are some things to "plan" concerning your return:

   o **Personal debrief with your pastor** concerning your pre-trip plan; the goals you set, your involvement while away, etc. Talk about how it went vs. how you expected it to go. Did it meet/exceed your expectations? Were there any disappointments? Will your involvement in the local church remain the same or change as a result of the trip – ie. Have you acquired new skills that you'd like to put to work in a different ministry locally? How will you work to preserve some of what God taught you while away? (This meeting should happen within 2 weeks of your return.)

   o **A Post-trip Service**: If the local church has supported you in any way, you should plan a service where you can share what happened during your tip: your activities, how God moved, what you learned, etc. Your goal is to thank them for their support and to encourage them that *through* their support, *they* have impacted the cause of missions. (If possible, this should happen within 3-4 weeks of your return).

o **6-month Check-in with your pastor:** Discuss how your first six months back have gone. If you've tried a new ministry, how's that going? Do you want to continue or try something new? Do you feel you've continued to grow in or have you regressed with respect to what God did in/for you during the trip? How are you doing in terms of your personal disciplines?

o **12-month Check-in:** Similar to the 6-month check-in, how have the last six months been going with regard to your goals, your relationship with God and the local church? Are you still on track? How are you "improving your serve"?

4. **Build your Team:** If yours will be a team trip and your sending organization communicates contact information for fellow team members, touch base with them individually. You can introduce yourself, say a word or two about what you're looking forward to and let them know that you'll be praying for them.

By doing this you begin, early on, to build a sense of community that can go a long way to improving the team dynamic when the group is finally assembled.

Electronic communication can facilitate this a great deal but something handwritten will make you stand out. Whatever medium you choose, make this initial reach-out personal and individual.

Challenge to Participants

STMers, the challenge for you is to overcome the

temptation to simply "relax" after the trip is over. You will be very intentional about preparations prior to departure and during your trip. I encourage you to not let your guard down upon returning home. Take the same level of intentionality and apply it to both your personal Christian walk and your public service in the local church. Many will have invested in you, wanting to see you succeed and grow in the long term. They believe in you. Work as unto the Lord… before, during and after your STM trip.

Audience #2:
Supporting Pastors & individuals

Pastors, since you are key gatekeepers in sending your people abroad, remind participants of recommendations in this chapter. The more you can encourage long-term growth in the life of each STM participant you commission and send into the harvest, the more you and your church (a) impact the Kingdom of God abroad and (b) stand to benefit from the training and faith-building opportunities afforded by STM. In addition, you will play a vital role in re-integrating volunteers back to the home church upon completion of their STM term. Don't leave re-integration to chance.

Pastors

I strongly encourage you to take a look at the "Plan your Return" section (immediately preceding this section). It is intended for the participant but it involves you as well. It encourages the participant to be intentional about their re-entry and to plan ahead in such a way as to maximize long-term personal change.

You can also reference the "Pastor's Checklist", found in the appendices at the back of the book.

Both of these tools pay tribute to the important role that you play in the development of STM participants before, during and after their trip. You're not just developing STM participants however, but sheep that Christ has entrusted to your care. Properly managed, the transition back into "day-to-day life" can help ensure that lasting positive change occurs. As that happens, and the closer you are to the process, the more you and your local church stand to gain from these ever-more equipped individuals. Together you are all better able to represent Christ in your city.

The one recommendation I would make to you, over and above what I've already laid out is this. If you have a STMer returning from a particular country, people or language group, it may be an opportunity to reach any of that population locally. It could begin as simply as inviting them to the service where your STMer presents the trip that they've just completed.

Pastors & Local Church Members

The Local church plays an essential role in nurturing the lives of young people long before they consider an STM opportunity. "More than simply communicating a missionary *vision*, [family & local churches] teach by example the *qualities* of a missionary life." (Friesen 2004, p.13)

You, more than anyone, are shaping the lives of future short-term missionaries. From your Sunday School classrooms, to your youth group, your ministry team are examples. You are among the earliest to model Christ to future STMers in how you approach the lost, the hurting and the vulnerable. You play a large role in the overall spiritual strength and health of participants.

Audience #3:
STM Sending Organizations

You play a vital role in linking STM candidates to countries, projects and missionaries that require helping hands. You are best-placed to have an overview of any evolving trends within your STMers base, projects, etc. Fine-tuning your observation and adaptability skills will allow you to react to these changes.

Here are a few specific recommendations that I would make for you:

1. **Debriefing:** When STMers return from any given field, there should be some form of standardized debriefing procedure. It could be as extensive as sit-down interviews with staff or, at the very least, a questionnaire (distributed while still abroad) where participants can capture significant observations, experiences, things they learned and things they wish they'd known before going. This is a granular approach to gathering information which may or may not make its way back 100% of the time. Over time however, trends will emerge that will allow the programs to be tweaked and pre-trip preparation to be improved. You'll need buy-in from both missionary personnel, STMers and office staff to gently but consistently point people to memorializing their feedback.

2. **Cultural Introduction:** Develop a "Top 10 List" of helpful cultural must-knows, according to countries or regions, for STM participants. It need not be exhaustive but could be a starting point for them to then take away and research more fully on their own. The best sources of information for such a list would be (a) previous STMers to that

country or region and (b) onsite missionaries. I deliberately place onsite missionaries second because their experience of the country is from the perspective of a long-termer. Previous STMers will have learned things in the context of a short term and will be aware of what they knew or did not know. To be clear however, input from both sources is ideal.

3. **Historical Context:** Develop a document for each STM destination over viewing the history of the organization's involvement there and the growth of the work that they'll be part of. It need not be encyclopedic but should provide key people, places and events in the history of the church there. It could be administered prior to or upon arrival in the country. This is less essential for 1-2 week STM trips but is of proportional importance for longer stays.

4. **Measurability:** It's important for STMers to feel that their time, effort and sacrifice is making positive change to the work in a given field. One thing that will help with that is to have clearly defined, measurable goals. There should be a process in place for regular evaluation between missions staff and STMers where both are able to evaluate what's going well (celebrate accomplishment) and tweak what could use improvement. This ensures that STMer involvement is a positive experience for all concerned.

5. **Shared contact & learning:** Remember that national Christians appreciate as much contact as possible with STMers. Whether doing outreach, construction work, or simply eating... be sure to engineer those times in such a way as to maximize contact-opportunities between the two groups.

Including nationals in an "on-the-field debrief session" where possible also give each group a chance to affirm the other by expressing how they've impacted one another.

6. **Keeping Contact:** Remember how Friesen indicated that those who've done multiple trips have a greater tendency to long-term change? Keeping some sort of contact with former STMers represents an opportunity both for you and for them:

  o **For you:** If you consider STM to be the "mouth of the funnel" so-to-speak, in terms of missionary recruitment, then as individuals do repeated trips, they move through the funnel and may eventually feed your long-term missions program.

  o **For them:** By maintaining some level of contact, even through social media for example, you regularly present them with new opportunities for participation. After having gone once, you become their trusted facilitator of all things missions. If and as they do repeat trips, it further anchors long-term change in their lives.

I'm not sure exactly what this ongoing contact looks like, but if structured and managed properly it allows you to build an incredible base for future mobilization.

APPENDICES

Recommended Reading:

Poitras, James G. and Howell, Bruce A. *(2012)* "Sensing God's Direction", Pentecostal Publishing, Hazelwood MO (www.PentecostalPublishing.com)

Works Cited:

Friesen, Randall Gary *(2004)*, Thesis summary of "Improving the Long-Term Impact of Short-Term Missions", unpublished doctoral thesis for the University of South Africa. *(available for download at www.MBMission.org)*

Taylor, William Vaughan *(2012)*, "Short-Term Missions: Reinforcing Beliefs and Legitimizing Poverty", Master's Thesis, University of Tennessee, Knoxville.

VerBeek, Kurt Alan *(2006)*, The Impact of Short-Term Missions – A Case Study of House Construction in Honduras after Hurricane Mitch, *Missiology: An International Review*, Vol 34, No 4, October 2006, pp. 477-496.

VerBeek, Kurt Alan *(2008)*, Lessons from the Sapling: Review of Quantitative Research on Short-Term Missions. In *Effective Engagement in Short-Term Missions: Doing it Right!* (edited by Robert Priest, William Carey Library), pp. 469-496.

COMMUNICATIONS CHECKLIST

For a 1-6 week STM trip,
I'd recommend the following.

☐ Introduction Letter & Video (2-3min max, get pastor's help and include your social media info)
☐ Financial Partner Card (PIM form)
☐ Customized note/post card to invite/thank.
☐ Bookmark – something that they can keep handy
☐ Facebook personal profile. (to house the video and make regular updates.
☐ 1 photo that tells a story is better than the last 35 photos on your phone's camera roll.

STM of a couple of months or longer
(in addition to above)

☐ Email List (for updates via email)
☐ Facebook Page (for updates separate from your personal profile.)
☐ Bookmark or prayer cards as a daily reminder for supporters.
☐ BLOG: Wordpress.com sites are easy & free
☐ Occasional video content.
☐ Personal communication (short notes/letters)
☐ Vary social media use (not everyone is on twitter)
☐ Skype, Video Chat, Facebook Live all open up many new opportunities for fast communication.
☐ Written submissions to district publications.

CHOOSING WHERE TO GO
(Based on Chapter 4)

Below are some questions to help you determine where God may be opening an STM door for you. This will be most useful if you are looking at STM involvement for the first or second time. With greater experience comes more ease in identifying opportunities about which God is stirring you.

Has God clearly spoken about a country / opportunity? *(if no... continue on to the other questions.)*

_____

What 1-2 week or 1-2 month opportunities are available?

_____

_____

_____

Am I a better fit to one of those options due to language?

_____

Do I have a particular interest in one of those options?

_____

Knowing other people (whether missionaries or other STM participants) associated with a given option may be a deciding factor but don't be afraid to "go it alone" and join with a team where you don't know anyone already. You already have something in common with them... a burden for missions.

147

PRAYER CHECKLIST
(Based on Chapter 5, **Praying for**...)

Yourself; that God would prepare you...

- [ ] To learn, both from people in the host country and from himself.
- [ ] To deal with any unforeseen things that arise.
- [ ] To be a giver: giving encouragement, giving a testimony, giving a great example.

The country to which He's called you

- [ ] Become aware of what's going on in that country spiritually, politically and socially. Pray that God gives you wisdom and discernment to minister in that specific context.

The missionaries with whom you'll be working

- [ ] Mine current and past communication from them *(blogs, newsletters, etc.)* to see what they've been facing and how God's already been moving. They may mention specific requests as well.

The events & projects with which you'll be involved.

- [ ] There will be things you expect to do as well as unplanned ministry moments. Pray that you will always be ready to minister through His Spirit.

Generally...

- [ ] For discernment
- [ ] For your family back home
- [ ] An open mind to new directions in which God may desire to lead you.

PASTOR'S CHECKLIST

Prior to STM Departure:

- [ ] Meet with them a few times in preparation, to:
  - o Review the application before submission.
  - o Discuss *their* hopes/expectations/goals.
  - o Discuss *your* hopes/expectations for them.
  - o Check-in on financial progress.
  - o Review last-minute questions or details.
- [ ] Have a commissioning service; they go with your blessing, representing Christ, you & the church.

While Away:

- [ ] Check in with them personally on a regular basis with these three questions:
  - o What have you been doing?
  - o How are you feeling?
  - o What is God teaching you?
- [ ] Video conference call during service time *(if away 1 month or more)*, where they greet the church and give an update. If "live" is not possible, they can pre-record and send a 5 minute cell phone video.

Upon Return:

- [ ] **Within 10 days:** Personal follow-up meeting to review pre-trip goals & expectations.
  - o Begin planning a church service where they present their trip to the local church.
  - o Get them thinking about re-entry into local church ministry: Are they wanting to try something different?
- [ ] **Within 1 month:**
  - o Have service where they present their trip.
  - o Get a firm decision on future ministry involvement. Present new options as 6-

month trial, to be revisited later.

☐ **Within 6th month:** Have a second debriefing session, similar to the first, and ask the following:

    o How have they been feeling since their return *(now that more time has passed)*?

    o Revisit any hopes/expectations that they shared previously.

    o What has been difficult or challenging about re-adjusting to "home"? *(This will be more important the longer their time away.)*

    o How do they feel about any new ministry assignments locally? Are they working out alright or do they need to be re-visited?

    o How has their personal walk been since returning?

☐ **Within 12th month:** Repeat the 6-month interview to follow-up and try to help them discern future ministry involvement.

Dear Pastor, if you will work through this checklist with your STM participant you will be seen as the "crème de la crème" and will go a long way to ensure that they experience long-term growth from their time away.

Your close follow-up ensures that the participant grasps the gravity of what they're embarking on. It also communicates that in addition to you desire to see them have the best possible STM experience, you also desire to see the local church benefit from their experience.

*** Follow-up communicates care. ***

The Final Word

*"Within the broader call to a life of mission,
there are many acts of obedience
with a particular purpose and time-frame
which, when viewed in isolation,
appear short-term"*

Randall Friesen

ABOUT THE AUTHOR

Mike participated in his first Short Term Missions trip in 1983. Just barely into his teen years at that point, his continued participation in STM endeavors, throughout his teens, planted in him a keen awareness of the difference a young person could make. He also became aware of the difference that such experiences could make in him.

He participated in several other STM trips during his twenties and went on hiatus as "daily life" kicked in after his marriage and during his kids' toddler years. He and his family were never on hiatus from ministry in the local church however and like Paul & Barnabas, it was as they served that God sent them out again, this time to France, where they have been since 2015. He blogs regularly about his family's STM work at **www.AIMLong.ca**.

He believes fiercely in the value of STM experiences for establishing young people and grounding them in a life of Christian service. He should. He is the product of STM.

* * *

(UPCI Global Missions account: #171805)

ONE LAST THING

If you've enjoyed this book and found it useful, I'd be very grateful if you'd post a short review on Amazon.

Your support really does make a difference and I read all reviews personally in order to get your feedback and make future updates book even better.

Thank you
…for purchasing this book. In doing so, you've helped us fund our STM work.

If you're considering STM yourself… May God give you

Short-Term Missions Success
Defining Moments Toward Long-Term Growth

#STMSuccess

Also by Mike Long

The Amazon #1 Hot New Release:

Paris 3 Days No Stress
A Travel Guide

*Are you, a friend or someone you know planning a trip to Paris? …
Let me help you with that.*

*This 120 page guide will give you top-level information on how to
navigate Paris' largest international airport as well as the public
transportation options. It will direct you toward 9 of the must-see
sights and activities as well as give you tips on how to experience the
city by creating memorable moments that won't break your budget.*

Available on Amazon
(in paperback & kindle versions)

Made in the USA
Coppell, TX
21 October 2020

40069902R00095